run_
frictionless

> HOW TO **FREE** A FOUNDER
FROM A **SALES** ROLE

TOLD BY ANTHONY COUNDOURIS

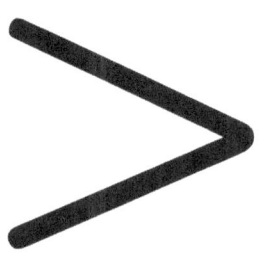

IN THE PAST MAN HAS BEEN FIRST; IN THE FUTURE THE SYSTEM MUST BE FIRST

FREDERICK W TAYLOR,
SCIENTIFIC MANAGEMENT 1911

COPYRIGHT © 2018 BY ANTHONY COUNDOURIS

All rights reserved. This book or any portion thereof may not be reproduced or used in any manner whatsoever without the express written permission of the publisher except for the use of brief quotations in a book review. For permission requests, write to the publisher at the address below.

Although the author and publisher have made every effort to ensure that the information in this book was correct at press time, the author and publisher do not assume and hereby disclaim any liability to any party for any loss, damage, or disruption caused by errors or omissions, whether such errors or omissions result from negligence, accident, or any other cause. Some names and identifying details have been changed to protect the privacy of individuals.

run_
frictionless

freethefounder@runfrictionless.com

Printed in the United States of America

Edition 1.6, 2020

ISBN 978-1-7315-9721-2

Kindle Direct Publishing

runfrictionless.com

ACKNOWLEDGMENTS

Thank you Sharon Dugan, without whose nighttime rescue in Helmsley, this book might never have been born.

Editing and proofreading by Rebecca Freeman. Developmental editing by Grant Butler, George Shaw, Michael Gormly and Barbara Messer. Contributions from Steve Dana.

Inspired by Silicon Valley giants Steve Blank and Marc Andreessen.

ABOUT THE AUTHOR

Anthony has a decade of experience consulting to technology and software-as-service startups. Brands include salesforce.com, Google, SAP and IBM. He specializes in designing automated sales and marketing systems. He has consulted to SaaS vendors in the United Kingdom, Korea, Singapore, the Philippines, and Australia. Anthony has been a founder of two startups.

His first business, Firestarter, consulted on Facebook and iPad app development in South East Asia. The firm was acquired by Novus Media in 2010. He co-founded Futurebooks, an accounting firm servicing over 500 startups and ranked as Xero's number one reseller in Asia. When he's not working, Anthony enjoys racing sports bikes and sailing boats.

Find him at linkedin.com/in/anthonycoundouris/

CONTENTS

Some background before we begin	1
Eliminate friction with the 4Qs	17
Quadrant 1 who we serve	31
Quadrant 2 what we serve	61
Quadrant 3 who we are	87
Quadrant 4 how we serve	115
The 4Qs in action	157
Glossary + Endnotes	186

SOME BACKGROUND BEFORE WE BEGIN

A company's first employee is its founder. When you, the founder, are the sole employee, controlling the brand and message is easy. You keep it inside your head and change the brand and message on the fly, depending on the audience who comes in contact with you.

In the beginning, you have few customers to manage. If two customers contact you five times daily, that's 10 customer interactions you manage each day or one interaction per hour.

As the business expands, so does the number of customers. Two customers become 10. They don't just call or email like before – now they contact you via online chat, SMS, and a few other channels. The number of customer interactions increases from 10 to 100 per day – a ten-fold increase.

You hire a salesforce, support people, and bring on sales partners. You are no longer on every call or attending every meeting. Instead of managing the customer interactions, it is now the staff who are in charge of delivering the brand and message.

As you add headcount, a headache erupts. No matter how many times you explain the brand and message, it becomes lost in translation. Some staff quote old prices, others promise features from future releases and partners write and use their own sales collateral, attracting the wrong types of customer.

Quality drops and the revenue expected doesn't arrive. The startup wins a few accounts, but no-one can explain why a sale was won or lost. Seeing the chaos, you work twice as hard. You skip the holidays you promised yourself and jump back onto sales. Instead of focusing on your executive role, you're involved in every customer interaction.

People don't get paid on time. There are no peer reviews. Staff birthdays are missed and not celebrated. This behavior drives a wedge between the founder and the organization because only sales count. The organization looks healthy because sales targets are met, but inside the company is crumbling. It appears the founder will never be free of their sales role.

In large organizations, a similar problem exists. A few high performing salespeople outperform the remaining salesforce. The process by which they achieve the results often remains a secret only they know. These salespeople are reluctant to share deals with others from the salesforce either because top salespeople lack the skill to teach or because they are afraid others will lose the customer.

What is missing is a system to free the founder and high performing salespeople. Let's call this a sales system. A sales system decodes the process of making a customer. A sales system spells out the ingredients or formula to make a customer, in a clearly understood sequence.

Imagine you're able to distil customer creation into a handful of interactions. For an internet startup, customer creation might look like three emails, two videos, a telephone call and a shout-out on Twitter. For a medical practice, the lineup might look like one messenger chat, one online booking, one interaction at an unmanned reception and one feedback form.

In either case, as long as staff follow the formula, you can predict the odds of creating a customer. The selling becomes intellectual property. It is the sales system that does the selling. One person is no longer responsible for taking a sale from A to Z. Each salesperson need only understand the part of the system where they contribute.

As the salesforce contributes to part of the sales system, you're also less likely to feel the vacuous effects of a salesperson leaving the company. If they decide to impart knowledge to a competing firm, their actions present a limited threat.

> MEET YOUR REPLACEMENT: THE SALES SYSTEM

The mistake founders and high performing salespeople make is trying to replace themselves with another human. Simply, there isn't another human like you looking for a job. Those who are like you are busy doing their own startup, not working for you. Here's how this "hire my replacement" story plays out.

You hire Jack. Jack sits next to you, follows you on the road, meets you after work, and has coffee with you and your family in the morning having spent the night on your living room floor. Jack is doing all the right stuff. But Jack never sells more than you do. Why? Because Jack is not a chef, he is a cook. Jack can bake a cake, not write the recipe to bake the cake. If Jack could write a recipe, he'd be a founder of a startup too.

So rather than hand Jack a list of ingredients, quantities to measure out and the length of time for each step, Jack sits beside you and is expected to learn through osmosis. Geeks call it pattern recognition.

> **He'll just pick it up. Soak it up like a sponge.**

The more coffee you have together, you think, the more he learns.

But he doesn't. After three months the sales figures are worse, so you fire Jack, and you hire Jill. You repeat the cycle all over again, never comprehending that you're the problem.

You've set Jack and Jill up to take a big fall. They could never be like you. If they were, they wouldn't be working for you.

We want to free the founder or sales team with a system, not a person. To quote Frederick W. Taylor, from his book Scientific Management, 1911:

> **In the past, man was first, in the future the system must be first.**[1]

In February 2016, I was asked by a software company to visit the U.K. and create a sales system for a payroll business. The organization had a high performing salesperson (let's call him Ed) who regularly sold more than the rest of the salesforce combined.

Over a two-week period, we recorded and listened to Ed's dialogue with customers. We read his email correspondence and we held many in-depth interviews with him. We quickly decoded why Ed sold more product.

Our research found that Ed had created 70 different customer interactions to help make a sale. Ed could weave a story to appeal to any customer profile. He plucked the most effective scripts and wove them into a narrative. When he discovered cases for which his script fell short, he scripted more.

Here is what Ed taught us:

A > You'll never hire Ed again. Ed is a writer, director and actor. He plays many roles. Being a capable individual, Ed is either a founder in his own startup or he is working for an enterprise business on megabucks.

B > No single individual will be responsible for making the entire sale. There were too many customer interactions to get right. It is wiser to train Ed's replacements to be specialists, each handling different legs of the customer journey.

C > There are too many customer interactions to manage. If we were ever going to create a predictable sale, we had to reduce the number of interactions from 70 to a more realistic number.

Sales systems bring a host of benefits other than scaling out a founder or sales team. If you try to acquire a customer without a sales system, you won't learn much. If you don't close the sale, you won't understand why, and if you close the sale you may also never know why. Either way, it's a dumb sale. You neither learned why they bought or didn't buy. Had you a sales system, you could improve and make the next sale you win or lose, predictable.

> SELL WHEN THE SALESFORCE IS NOT AT THEIR DESK

Automation moves the customers through the sales system even when the salesforce or founder is not at their desk. A sales system does the heavy lifting and repetitive tasks.

Rather than writing hundreds of bespoke emails, scripted email templates can be used, requiring only small changes to customize them to the needs of each customer. Document collection once handled manually, is taken care of by online forms that deliver the files in one single package. Repetitive operations like these once performed by the salesforce are replaced by the sales system, freeing the salesforce to concentrate on high-value tasks.

The applications which support the sales system and serve words and pictures, once custom-built and maintained on-premise, are available from the cloud. Since 2011, the number of marketing and sales applications has grown from 150 to 5,000 in 2017[2].

There is no limit to how these applications can be plugged, coupled and connected.

> WHY STARTUPS BECOME FOLLOWERS NOT LEADERS

Perhaps the most astounding benefit of a sales system is the opportunity to become a market leader. That means it can not only free a founder from a sales role, it can outperform the founder. Now that the sale is a liberalized process, more people in the business can contribute to making a sale. More minds equal more ideas. A sales system can become a means of out-performing the founder or a high-performance salesforce.

The value of a sale is improved. When a founder makes a sale, the value of the sale is low, because their time was used. A sale becomes valuable when the sale is made by another.

By decoding the founder and structuring a sale into a recipe, more minds can go to work each day, improving the sales system. Rather than improving individual sales techniques, the salesforce is orientated to think about how to improve the system. Every improvement raises the effectiveness of every salesperson.

In 2018 we asked founders from internet startups how they created words and pictures to communicate what their startups offered customers. Words and pictures include value propositions, benefit statements, about us pages – everything that appears in a company's sales collaterals.

Other than the founder's own experience, common sources of intel that shape words and pictures included:

A > Colleague's experience

B > Competitor's experience

C > Agency experience

What struck me about the findings was how blasé founders were when it came to deciding how to craft words and pictures. Their approach is rather like a student, cramming the night before an essay is due.

The starting point does not rest on a foundation, .ie., anything unique within your business.

It is fine to gather intelligence from your competitor, but it is another thing entirely to steal their words and pictures. It is not sustainable because you have no basis from which to improve. Operationally, you may never be able to deliver on their value propositions because every company is built differently. They have different shareholders, a different company culture and different staff. You may also consider the act unethical.

> WORDS + PICTURES MATTER

The decision about what words and pictures will look like is frightfully important. Granted, the creation of words and pictures is iterative.

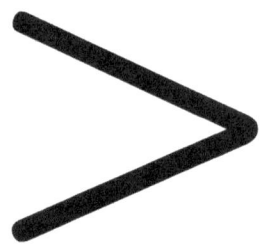

You are not wedded to it forever and it can change, like veneer.

I think of words and pictures as a veneer because a veneer describes how easy and cost-effective it is to change. A veneer is great at masking imperfections found on the surfaces of walls. Have you ever noticed how striking a room can appear just by changing the color on a wall? Take a room that is dull and change one wall and it can light up the whole room.

So words and pictures matter. What you stake today is what you will be judged upon. Staff, customers, shareholders and the media each read your words and pictures and make up their minds about the sort of company you are.

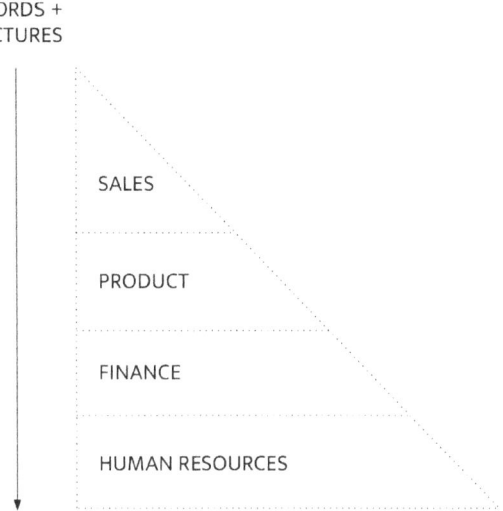

They'll decide if this is an all too familiar story – something they have heard regurgitated a hundred times. They'll decide if this is completely new, get excited, wowed and talk about it. Or maybe it's an idea before its time.

Either way, you'll be labeled as a follower or leader. A copycat or an innovator.

> ONCE A FOLLOWER, ALWAYS A FOLLOWER

If you perpetuate this decision-making pattern in the first few years of operation, what is to stop you from repeating it in the third, fourth and fifth year?

After all, you've taught both yourself as founders and the organization to think this way. You taught them to follow.

The pattern of following begins with words and pictures and cascades down into every facet of the business. This is because the entire business is connected to whatever promises you make in words and pictures. Operations, finance, product development: they all fall like dominoes.

That's because words and pictures contain value propositions. Value propositions are promises you make to customers. When you sell a product you have to deliver what you promised, so the entire organization is now following.

It is easy to see why the majority of startups begin as followers and remain followers.

In the U.K. there is a sector of the economy called umbrella companies. An umbrella company is a fancy name for firms that provide shared services like payroll, insurance and loans to working contractors. In 2016 we friction tested this sector and benchmarked the top five competing sales systems. We discovered all five mimicked the same interaction when contacting a customer for the first time. In fact, each competitor even called this interaction by the same name. They called it a "pay illustration". A pay illustration is a table of figures that tell a contractor what their take-home salary is, less fees, etc. While the figures vary, the layout is much the same. Figures arranged in columns, exported from a spreadsheet, dumped verbatim in an email and shot out to a customer.

From the research, we inferred the words and pictures, created by competitors, were a copy of a copy of a copy. These competitors were a bunch that made incremental changes based on each other's incremental changes. This type of decision-making involves no decision-making. One simply follows a competitor's actions.

If you're a startup moving into an industry of followers, you can do a lot of damage. If you are one of the followers, you're more vulnerable than you know. Remember, customers judge startups on words and pictures. What you present is what you're judged upon.

Rather than picking up intel and shoving it directly into words and pictures like the umbrella companies did, I would like you to use the 4Qs as a decision-making framework – one where you can use what intel you gather from those around you, not as gospel, but as a guide.

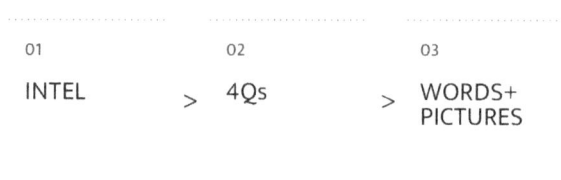

Instead of following, your startup will create unique words and pictures, because rather than follow, you synthesize intelligence gathered. If you create unique words and pictures you will, by design, become a market leader.

Even if you never become a market leader by claiming a majority market share, your startup will exemplify the decision-making pattern of a market leader. You avoid the trap of becoming blinkered by watching incremental decisions made by others. You will think about whether you should act on intelligence, and how. Your decision-making will be based upon a foundation, from which new decisions can be measured.

> REJOICE WHEN COMPETITORS STEAL YOUR WORDS + PICTURES

The 4Qs protect your words and pictures even when your competitors flatter you by unashamedly stealing them. After all, if founders borrow words and pictures from others, you can expect this will be done to you.

Your competitors will make the mistake of stealing words and pictures and become followers. However, they will not understand the logic behind the choice of words and pictures, or what decision is coming next, because they only see the veneer. Words and pictures can be stolen, but the 4Qs and the intelligence behind the 4Qs are safe, tucked away from spying eyes in the public domain.

If you make one iteration to words and pictures each day, you can improve 20 times in one month or 240 times in a year (assuming 20 workdays per month). If a competitor mystery shops you today, it will take them at least 30 days to implement changes to their words and pictures.

Over the period of a year, you are ahead most days. Maybe they steal from you three or four times per year. They are unlikely to repeat the process often because it is time-consuming. When they do steal, they cannot iterate fast enough.

Your startup, judged on words and pictures, is regarded as a leader. The competition responds by doing what they did yesterday, by following, and you – with your intelligence within your 4Q framework – will always be at least one step ahead.

In the next chapter, we explore the 4Qs and how the 4Qs framework can turn your company into a market leader.

ELIMINATE FRICTION WITH THE 4Qs

There are plenty of tactical things you can do as a founder to free yourself from a sales role. A good tip is to begin recording all your calls and writing down in a script document key emails you repeatedly send out.

These types of tips and tricks won't be covered in this book.

Instead, I'm going to teach you a more robust method. I design and build sales systems for enterprises and startups across Asia Pacific. I've been doing this for a number of years. Each time I start a new gig I'm given three months to show results.

So when I'm trying to free a founder or a sales team, I use the framework I designed called the 4Qs. I first began writing about the 4Qs two years ago as a teaching aid I could hand out to clients. I have rolled out the 4Qs to countless organizations. It's my hope you learn the basics and walk away and implement the 4Qs in your startup. I have not been able to find a better framework.

The power of the 4Qs rests in its ability to create four, distinct quadrants, or windows, into an organization, such that all its people and processes can be grouped into one or more quadrants. The 4Qs educate people about how their role and processes touch a customer. Let's take a closer look at the 4Qs.

Q1 WHO WE SERVE	Q2 WHAT WE SERVE
Q3 WHO WE ARE	Q4 HOW WE SERVE

Q1 addresses whom you serve today and whom you serve tomorrow. The remaining three quadrants deal with what you are serving the customer, what you share in common with the customer, and how it feels to become a customer of your startup.

> DOWNLOAD FREE 4QS PLAYBOOK

Our playbook will teach you how to play or fit one Quadrant with another. Alternatively, you can access 4Qs templates from popular template sharing sites. Visit runfrictionless.com or point your camera phone at the QR code.

> RUNNING FRICTIONLESS

It is important when building out your picture of the 4Qs that you remain sensitive to the presence of friction. Every sales system, no matter how well-designed, presents the customer with friction.

Friction slows the customer from reaching their goal, and equally slows the sale.

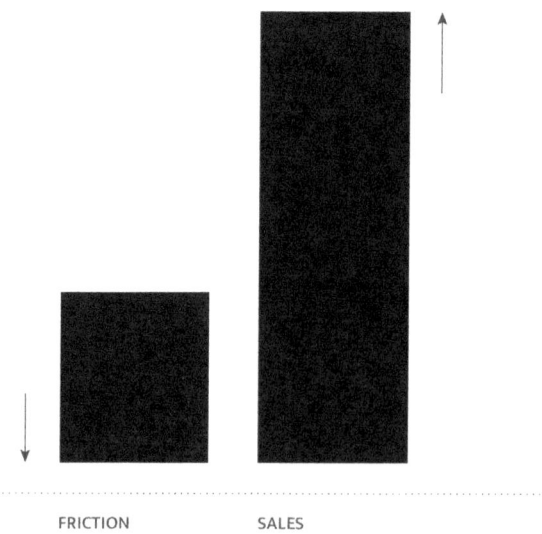

Friction points are where customers get stuck in a sales system, either because they don't understand what to do next or what is being demanded of them is too time-consuming.

In trying to serve the company's own needs, the company creates friction which causes customers to drop-off. Drop-off is when a customer delays or abandons their goal, due to overwhelming friction. Think about a difficult interaction you've had as a customer. You delay or abandon your goal. You quit. You walk off and forget you ever wanted the product.

Drop-off is more likely to be avoided when the following equation is satisfied.

By reducing friction, a buying decision is effortless for the customer. It feels like a natural, wonderful experience, where every detail has been considered and no thinking is required on the part of the customer.

I will paint a literal example of friction. I was sitting inside a cafe sipping a coffee one morning. It was quiet, there were not a lot of customers around. I couldn't see the barista, but I knew they were not far.

From behind the counter, I could hear someone casually gaming on a mobile phone.

I had a full view of the passing street traffic and noticed a man and his partner approach. They considered the words and pictures on the menu and decided to enter. He pushed on the door, but it didn't yield. So he pushed harder. It made a noise that suggested, "please don't do that again".

To my astonishment, the visitor about-faced and returned to the street, presumably to search for an alternative. I found the incident rather amusing, as I'd fallen prey to the same trick. Pushing on a door that was meant to be pulled. Or pulling when you were supposed to push.

This example can teach us a lot about friction. Let's cast the visitor as a customer and the glass door as a customer interaction – all of which are part of a much bigger sales system. I imagined this was running through the mind of the customer:

> Well, if it's this hard to get into the place, imagine how uninspiring it will be to order a plate of food.

Crossing through the front door is a key interaction. It represents the customer shifting from the public to the retail space and signaling their desire to move closer to a buying decision. Faced with friction, the customer dropped off.

The door opens in one direction. Assuming whether a customer push or pull on the door is decided on a coin toss, 50 percent of customers will encounter friction. Of the 50 percent who experience friction, a significant number will drop off.

> ELIMINATE FRICTION

Let's see how the business owner of the restaurant intends to eliminate friction.

A > Add a label to the door that reads "Pull". This is a good start. A label names the limits of the door. The only problem is this relies on the customer to read the label. This particular restaurant is internationally renowned and many customers do not speak English.

The business owner notices that when they name limits, it doesn't eliminate friction. So they try plan B.

B > They place a human being outside the front door. As the customer approaches the door, a staff member opens the door for them. This is a common fix for friction and one I see used often in shopping malls in S.E. Asia. Either because the computer processor is slow or the listings are not intuitive, a person stands beside the directory board and operates the kiosk on your behalf to help find your destination.

This is effective at reducing friction and customer visits at the restaurant rise. However it's expensive to maintain and when the staff member is in a restroom or on leave, the friction is back.

C > Replace the door with a bi-directional door. The proprietor, having tried to name limits and throw humans at the problem, now decides to design the friction out of the sales system. They will make an investment and replace the door with a new door that opens bi-directionally.

Drop-off decreases and the restaurant experiences more orders. The label which named limits is removed and this valuable real estate is used to announce the restaurant's TripAdvisor rating. However, the glass door is heavy and opening it requires some strength. Time for plan D.

D > Introduce automatic doors. The business owner automates the entire interaction. The experience is contactless. The door has a sensor that detects when a customer is near and opens the door for them. Friction eliminated. Or is it?

Six months later a startup restaurant selling similarly priced chicken opens in proximity to the restaurant. Instead of automatic doors, the startup designs the shop front such that no door is required. They combine the outdoor and indoor space together by introducing an open plan.

They completely eliminate the customer interaction, and therefore the burden of managing the interaction. Startups that run frictionless have an insatiable appetite for designing friction out from the business.

> FRICTION HAS A QUOTIENT

There is another dimension of friction you need to understand. Friction accumulates. Customers remember the friction they experience from one interaction to the next.

If you benchmark your sales system against competing sales systems, theoretically you can attach to each a friction score. The larger the number, the greater the friction. A company with a score of 5 is doing better than a company with a score of 8.

Therefore any reduction of friction in a sales system will improve overall performance because customers remember.

> ❝ I just want to know where kitchenware is!

The purpose of a sales system is not to save a company time and money. The aim is not to make the sales system efficient but to help the customer achieve their goal in the shortest possible time.

Trying to be efficient is a fast way to friction. The company's goal becomes an obstacle and blocks the customer from achieving their goal. Start a dialogue with a customer, the way they want to. You are competing not only with sales systems designed by other businesses, but a more sinister and unseen enemy called customer expiry.

Website gimmicks like pop-ups that demand a visitor's email address don't create customers, they turn customers away. Blocking a customer from achieving their goal infuriates them. So often we demand a customer give us a bunch of particulars before we agree to serve them.

Consider a customer – let's call her Sally – walks into the supermarket.

 Sally: Can you tell me which aisle I can find kitchenware?

Sales assistant (blank-faced, slowly replies): Before I can speak to you I need your name and email address.

Sally: I just want to know where kitchenware is! Surely I don't have to give you my life history?

Sales assistant: Sorry. I need your name and email before I can speak to you.

Sally: But you are speaking to me.

> **Sales assistant:** That's beside the point. I need your name and email.

At some point during the dialogue, it may become necessary to take the customer's name and email address to facilitate answering their inquiry. Raise it only if it is required – don't add friction.

All of us have experienced moments when a company's efficiency is prioritized above our goal. An example that comes to mind is check-in kiosks at airports. Airlines have recently introduced these devices to improve efficiency. The kiosk demands you input a passport and flight number. What the kiosk design is blind to is the fact that customers are often holding bags and don't have the fingers to touch type. Customers like me must be thinking:

❝ Great, thanks for adding friction.

> Time is an important dimension to making a buying decision. Every customer goal has an expiry. If the goal is not achieved in the time frame, the customer is likely to drop off and abandon their buying decision.

> When a customer enters into a buying decision, assume they are evaluating a few competitors. It is wise to think of making a sale as a race to achieve the customer's goal before a competitor.

> YOU'RE MORE LIKELY TO MAKE A SALE

By putting the customer's goal first, you are more likely to make a sale compared to your competitor.

In many industries buying decisions take a long time not because the products are high involvement, but because friction points create inefficiency in the buying decision. I've heard suppliers criticize decision-makers from enterprise companies as slow when making a buying decision. I don't entirely agree that it is the fault of the enterprise. These organizations want to buy your product. However, these companies face so much friction evaluating suppliers they often abandon their goal.

Remove the friction from the customer experience, and buying decisions that once took four months can be compressed into a single month.

> IT'S JUST TOO HARD

Customer complaints or poor customer reviews often stem from friction. The goal of the sales system deviates from the customer's goal and the customer begins to think their time is wasted. Common expressions of frustration include:

❝ It's too hard.

❝ I'm too busy.

You hear yourself and your staff remark:

❝ I feel like we're going in circles.

That's friction. Friction is any obstacle that slows the customer from reaching their goal and equally slows the company from making a sale. What typifies friction is a period of time when a startup cannot turn a single customer, and sales are unpredictable. If we hold talent, culture and investment constant, a startup's ability to overcome friction can be the deciding factor as to whether the startup will succeed or not.

Here are activities that typify friction and frictionless.

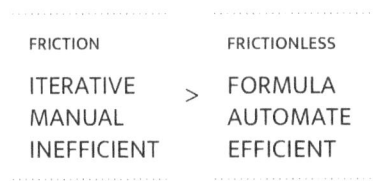

FRICTION		FRICTIONLESS
ITERATIVE	>	FORMULA
MANUAL		AUTOMATE
INEFFICIENT		EFFICIENT

It is a good idea to keep these lessons on friction firmly in your mind, as we begin now building out a picture of what the 4Qs will look like in your business.

ANTHONY COUNDOURIS

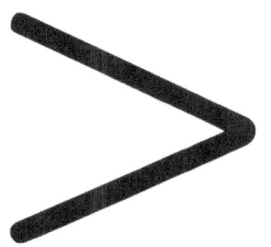

QUADRANT 1 WHO WE SERVE

Awesome. You've turned the page and bought into why we need the 4Qs.

The first quadrant is the cornerstone of the 4Qs. Until you understand to whom you are speaking, none of the remaining quadrants make sense. You will sell into a vacuum where no-one is paying attention to your brand, because you are not speaking to any one person specifically.

The decisions made in Quadrant 1 affect the decisions made in other quadrants. For example, if you decide to position your firm to an enterprise customer, it will change the course of the product roadmap in Quadrant 2, and it will affect the shared beliefs created in Quadrant 3. The customer flow you built-in Quadrant 4 optimized for a small business is redundant because the decision-maker from an enterprise business has a different buying decision than a small business owner.

A common phrase I hear technical founders tell me is "anyone can buy the product." While that is true, it is not anyone you are trying to convince to buy. You're trying to convince one person, Sally, to buy, and Sally won't buy if Sally is not convinced the product is right for her.

Sally is not a target audience. She is an individual, and she is your customer. Putting a personal description to paper forces the organization to build products and sell them to an individual person. It is easy to educate the whole company about Sally when we have a description of Sally in writing.

One copywriter I knew kept a picture beside his desk of a person who embodied the customer profile. He didn't write copy for a target audience – he wrote to Sally. Having a clear picture of whom you are speaking to means you can empathize with your customer. If you cannot empathize with them you can never write words and pictures which resonate.

You'll want to store and share these customer profiles in a document where anyone in the business can refer

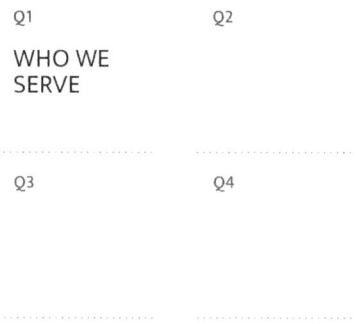

to it in the future. It is a document written by marketing people with input from the founder. The customer profile is a mutual understanding between the salesforce and customer service about who is allowed to become a customer.

The salesforce therefore is not evaluated on the basis of selling to anyone but selling to a specific customer profile.

It is empowering when the startup can choose its customer. When the business wins the customer you want, there is a reason to celebrate.

Apart from tracking the customer you serve, there are a few other profiles we need to keep an eye on. There are customers you don't serve, customers you serve tomorrow, customers you are compelled to serve and customers you serve through.

Let's begin with customers we don't serve today.

> CUSTOMERS YOU DON'T SERVE

In a startup, it is a relief to acquire any type of customer. A sale to any customer profile can be a sign the startup is on the right path. However seasoned founders know there is a toll exacted on the startup when serving the wrong profile. This profile does not provide worthwhile intel and at best tests the patience of your team.

It is your business and you are not obliged to serve everyone who fronts up on your doorstep. Deciding who to exclude is as important as who to include. The reason being that the more customer profiles you serve, the more you dilute competitive advantage in Quadrant 2 and 3. It is difficult to build rich feature sets and shared beliefs when you serve many kinds of customer profiles.

If you begin serving the wrong profile, you will be forced to eliminate these customers later, employ public relations professionals to mop up the bad press and unwind features from Quadrant 2 which are not relevant. This customer profile is a liability dressed as an asset.

One of the strongest reasons not to serve a customer profile is because the profile is unlikely to write a positive review. You predict they will have a negative experience. If you cannot imagine in the mind's eye the kind of positive review a customer will tweet after using your product, perhaps this customer profile is better served tomorrow or not at all. You cease serving a customer profile not because you don't like them, but because you cannot reach customer success. You are being honest and saying:

> ❝ Hey, don't come into our home. We know you won't like it.

It is important to define who we do not serve. When customer inquiries are coming thick and fast, the salesforce needs to make split-second decisions about who they ought to serve. By trying to serve everyone including those who they cannot serve or should serve tomorrow, they risk dropping customers who really need them and which they can serve today.

There are other reasons too. In situations where customers come together in a community, some customer profiles may not mix well with other types. For example, nightclub door staff regularly prevent the entry of customers. The door staff reserve the right to refuse entry because they realize one customer profile may dilute the experience for another customer they serve.

One simple, natural way to stop or deter a particular customer profile is to change the price in Quadrant 2. A shift up or down in price can create enough friction to prevent the customer making a purchase.

An increase in price will make price-sensitive profiles

look elsewhere to solve their goal. A decrease in price will make customers with high expectations look elsewhere.

For example, a customer who wants a quick, budget haircut may look for a new product if prices in a salon were raised 20 percent. An enterprise customer may stop knocking on the door of a consulting firm if prices of services plummeted by 40 percent as part of a strategy to move to self-service and target small businesses.

Another reason for turning away a customer is because operationally you're not able to serve the customer. A general ward in a hospital can treat victims with mild injuries. However, they do not have the equipment, the training or the kind of empathy to serve a customer in need of intensive care.

If you orient the staff around a particular shared belief, but bring into the business customer profiles who do not share that belief you are disrupting the staff and giving them a reason to leave the company.

In businesses that require cooperation from the customer in order to create customer success, decisions to shield the company from a profile is paramount. Many business models fall into this category – medical clinics treating rehab patients and web designers building websites for small business owners, all fall into a category where the outcome is connected to the customer's level of cooperation.

The more the profile cooperates, the greater their utility, and the greater the likelihood of a positive review.

- 🔓 Visit the glossary at the end of the book to find the meaning of "customer success" and other important terms.

- ▶ It's a good idea to watch a few 4Qs Insight videos while you read the book. These videos will help bring the book to life.

> CUSTOMERS YOU SERVE TOMORROW

There may be customer profiles that you are not economically able to serve today. However, you forecast they are likely to fit the 4Qs in the next 12–24 months because of changing circumstances in your company or in the market.

Perhaps their volume of consumption is too small to make a relationship with this profile profitable. They are casual rather than heavy users. Perhaps the cost of acquiring them puts this profile out of reach. Or maybe the profile requires customization of Quadrant 2 before the product provides enough utility.

Either way, this profile could derive some utility from your product. However rather than invite them into the business today and risk jeopardizing the relationship, you put this customer on a waiting list and serve them tomorrow. Here's how this dialogue could play out.

 Founder: OK. So I could sell you what we have today, but I know you won't like it. It will fall short of your expectation.

Sally: Oh dear, we really wanted to use your product today.

Founder: You will be the first to know as soon as we have the next release of the software live.

Sally: Thanks for being honest.

Founder: Give me your name, your number and email address and I'll call you tomorrow when we are ready to serve you.

By being honest about the startup's ability to service the customer today builds trust and creates a pipeline of sales.

> CUSTOMERS YOU ARE COMPELLED TO SERVE

Let's turn our attention to those customers we are compelled to serve. In the process of serving a customer, a startup may be inadvertently compelled to serve customers who are not buyers. A fintech startup serving loans to individuals who need short-term financing may be compelled to meet government licensing, policy and fair practice.

Internet startups with activities in regulated markets come under great scrutiny from government. The words and pictures they use to promote their product, their practices, and complaints filed by customers can draw action from government.

Satisfying this customer profile is essential if government deems your activities require regulation and a license to operate.

For example, during my tenure with a fintech startup, keyword research told us customers were twice as likely to keyword search for the term "lending", than "invoice finance" when looking for our product.

It makes more sense to use the "lending" in words and pictures because it presents less friction. However, government explicitly forbade using the word "lending" and required the fintech to hold a different license if it did. Fail to serve government, and the fintech may have their license revoked or the renewal declined.

The same fintech startup may also serve shareholders. Shareholders have invested money to start the fintech. Whether through an IPO, ICO or private sale, these individuals matter because they influence the company at a board level.

You cannot control where your value propositions will be shown. Value propositions in the public domain can easily be read by shareholders and government who may disapprove.

PhilPay, a provider of SaaS payroll in the Philippines, positioned their product as the Philippines' most compliant payroll.

While this shared belief won them favor with the government, it meant they could not serve every customer profile.

If the brand tried to, it would mean they would "bend the rules" for some profiles, and force compliance on others. This duplicity would never work.

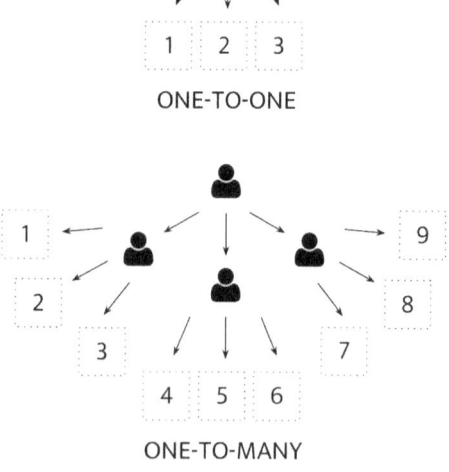

> CUSTOMERS YOU SERVE THROUGH

When SaaS flattened distribution, software resellers lost market share and closed shop. In their place grew a new kind of reseller, one that kept pace with SaaS. We call this new intermediary a Value-Add Reseller. I'll refer to this customer profile as a VAR.

VARs bring a customer base and have the trust of the customer base to sell new products. VARs are from all walks of services – lawyers, accountants, fitness trainers, taxi drivers and hairdressers.

It is not uncommon for a small accounting or law practice to have between 200 and 300 customers.

When a startup spends time developing a relationship with an end customer, the relationship is one-to-one. When a company spends the same amount of time with a VAR, they create a one-to-many relationship.

There is leverage in a one-to-many relationship. If a company has a relationship with three direct customers, they have created three potential sales. If a startup cultivated three relationships, each with a VAR, the number of sales could be as high as nine. That is threefold the sales compared to one-to-one.

One-to-many relationships demonstrate how quickly startups can grab market share by spending effort supporting and incentivizing VARs.

> CUSTOMERS YOU SERVE TODAY

Let's canvas the most important profile: the customer you serve today. I am perplexed by the phrase we hear business advisors give all the time: 80 percent of your business comes from 20 percent of your customers. Let's rewrite this advice.

100% of your business comes from 100% of your customers. This is what it means to choose the customer you serve today. Here's how we can achieve this.

One: decide to serve a single customer profile, and dominate this profile. The advantage of this is that the startup becomes known for something. It is difficult to build a story around Quadrant 3 if you're not creating customer success in at least one profile.

Two: targeting one profile at a time means limited resources are focused on a single target. Each customer profile you target has repercussions on Quadrants 2, 3 and 4. Quadrant 2 may suit any profile from Quadrant 1, however, you may not be able to operationally serve a customer profile in Quadrant 4 or create shared beliefs in Quadrant 3.

Trying to be all things to all profiles will dilute Quadrants 2, 3 and 4 and you risk serving no customers.

To illustrate this point we need to go back in time and analyze a friction test I conducted in 2016 on hairdresser salons in New South Wales, Australia. The findings would help Phorest, a SaaS company from Ireland, develop a go-to-market strategy in Australia. We profiled the industry in three: owner-operated salons, chain retailers and mobile hairdressers.

Profiling is the act of categorizing a customer into groups based on whichever data points are most significant. Marketing teaches that we profile according to age, sex, size etc. These are helpful but by no means the only data points. We profiled all three using several data points including expiry and intel.

After profiling, we decided to serve the owner-operated salons today. This was the largest profile, making up 90% of the market. Customer expiry was a few hours.

These decision-makers would sit at a PC of an evening after closing the salon, research and expect to close their buying decision in a single session. They had no time to shop around.

Chain retailers we would serve tomorrow. Chain stores delivered the highest ticket price because the money they spent did not belong to them personally. However, these firms were not necessarily the most profitable. They had long customer expiry, meaning we had more time to serve them, but on the flip side meant we had more customer interactions to manage. They had already made investments in building their own in-house proprietary systems, so switching was not critical.

Mobile hairdressers we decided never to serve. This group was the smallest and the most price-sensitive. The type of product features they needed was quite different compared with owner-operated salons.

It's 9pm in the evening and Sally is shopping online for a new cloud application to run her salon. Sally is an owner-operator of a hair salon. Here's how the dialogue plays out between Sally and the chat agent:

 Sally: I'd like to run my entire salon on your platform. Can I do this?

Chat agent: Yes. Tell me more.

	owner-operated	chains
size	large	small
expiry	a few hours	six months
value	must-have	nice-to-have
price sensitivity	high	low
touch	low	high
Intel	high	low
innovation	high	low
buying trigger	new financial year	unknown

Sally: Sure. We are using spreadsheets at the moment, and it's doing my head in. Only one person can log in at a time, and my staff forget to update the records.

Chat agent: Our product will solve that problem. I recommend you start on the middle package.

Sally: Seems expensive? Doesn't cost me anything at the moment.

Chat agent: When you add up the losses in productivity and potential theft of cash, it's actually cheap. Perhaps you need some time to consult your partners?

Sally: Nah. I make all the decisions around here. If I decide to go with you tonight, can we get started right away? I need it up and running by tomorrow.

Chat agent: Yes. Now is the best time to make the switch. It is the start of the new financial year.

Sally: OK. Let's do this.

Note how forthcoming Sally was explaining her problem to the chat agent. Customer profiles who willingly divulge intel make the next sale easier. Not every customer profile offers this type of intelligence. In a chain retailer there are many decision-makers, so gathering intel from each decision-maker is difficult.

> RUN THE NUMBERS

Deciding who you will serve, who you won't serve, who you will serve tomorrow, and those you are compelled to serve presents one of the most complex decisions a startup founder needs to make. The decision is multidimensional. Decisions made in Quadrant 1 will impact Quadrants 2, 3 and 4.

When we decided to serve owner-operated salons, we sanity checked our thinking by running the numbers. It is easy to fall prey to biases. Perhaps we have fallen in love with a particular customer profile and become too attached. Or we have fixated on the high ticket price attached to a customer profile and ignored the high cost to serve them.

When we started this chapter we could have titled Quadrant 1 "who you sell to." Instead, we chose the word "serve" instead of sell. Why?

Serve is a more realistic valuation because serve takes into account the cost of making a sale and the cost of serving a customer over the entire lifetime. Serve implies you are helping the customer to reach their goal, and achieve customer success. This is a far more expensive endeavor than to simply sell.

It is no longer acceptable to measure a startup's performance on a sale made or lost. Customer success is the new metric. That could be T+30 days. Transaction plus thirty days of customer success.

If you're confused deciding who to serve, beside each customer profile, list whether the customer is likely to leave a positive review. Be authentic. Focus on a customer's profile you can help today. Serving a customer profile that will never reach customer success is foolish.

To calculate which profile presents the least friction, run each profile by the following data points.

A > What price can you charge? The higher the price, the more chance you have to cover the cost of serving the customer.

B > Are they using their money or someone else's? When customers use their own money to buy your product, the greater the friction extracting the fee.

C > Can you satisfy the customer goal before expiry? If not, you are likely to receive negative reviews, even if the customer never bought. Small business owners have a simpler goal and the expiry date of their buying decision is quick compared to C-level employees procuring services on behalf of an enterprise.

D > How long or short is customer expiry? The longer customer expiry, the more customer interactions. The more interactions, the more points of friction. If the expiry is too short, you may not be able to serve fast enough.

E > Can you serve low-touch interactions? Some profiles may only need to be touched once per quarter. Other profiles may be high touch requiring attention once hourly. A high-touch customer will put more pressure on the support team than a low-touch customer.

F > Is your product a nice-to-have or a must-have product? A must-have product delivers a lot of value and is mission-critical. These customers tend to be heavy users, are more loyal and face higher switching costs. Nice-to-have products deliver relatively low value, sometimes attracting casual users who are less loyal.

G > How much experience do they require? Some products require domain experience in order for a customer to reach customer success. They may require onboarding. Other products work straight out of the box.

Until you net these expenses (and more), you cannot compare what it takes to serve a profile. Some profiles may begin to appear as liabilities, while others that appeared mediocre, begin to shine.

Before we move onto Q2, we are going to pay Sally one more visit. We are about to discover Sally is not as homogeneous as we first thought, and why we can predict when Sally will do before Sally knows.

> THIN SLICING ACCORDING TO ATTITUDE

We are going to re-examine who we serve. It turns out Sally is a bit more complicated.

If we thin slice customer profiles, we discover nuances competitors may have missed and therefore, new variants we can serve. Variants are created because one of the data points is significant enough to warrant that a profile be split into several variants.

Attitudes determine the way a customer profile sees their problem and solution the moment they make contact with a startup. The experiences variants have had trying to solve their problem in the last few hours, days or months matter. Variants may share similar problems but respond to different value propositions because their attitudes differ. The way they start their buying decision is different because each variant is in a different state of mind.

Let's revisit the salon friction test one more time. To the untrained eye, the owner-operator's attitude to their business has no bearing on a buying decision. However, after thin slicing, their attitudes were regarded as fundamental. Owner-operated salons were not homogeneous as we first thought. Instead of one profile, owner-operators were comprised of two variants.

We called variant one "entrepreneurs" and variant two "tax-optimizers". Entrepreneurs fell asleep each night dreaming of growing the brand and turning their business into a franchise. The entrepreneurial types were more likely to take a space in the CBD or eastern suburbs in Sydney, join associations, teach at local technical colleges and enter hair competitions. They were looking to make strategic investments that would give them an edge.

75% of owner-operated salons were tax-optimizers and took spaces in more suburban malls, and did not have aspirations of growing the business. Their pursuit was not to create the best haircut but maximize profits. The salon is less a business and more a lifestyle.

To isolate the two variants required that we thin sliced according to several data points. One significant data point we identified was whether the salon had adopted online bookings. We inferred that if the owner had already installed a booking engine, they were more likely to buy a SaaS product because they had already bought once from the category.

> VARIANTS WHO WELCOME CHANGE

Some variants are under pressure to change, and change is forcing these variants to make buying decisions. In other words, some variants are early adopters of new ideas – your idea. This is because variants have different attitudes to change.

They innovate not because it's cool, but because they have no choice. They innovate or they die. These variants have a higher propensity to make a buying decision. Other customer profiles are sitting on easy street and there is no pressure to change.

Here are a few conditions which put pressure on variants to change and adopt new ideas.

EXPANDING SECTORS ATTRACT NEW CUSTOMERS

Sectors that are expanding, rather than contracting, attract new customers. These new customers are startups and have no existing supplier relations. They are open to new ideas and want to avoid repeating what the existing competition has done. They often have no category experience. Being unsophisticated they come with no preconceived notions of what the product should look like. So there is less friction in asking this customer profile to adopt a new idea.

SECTORS EXPERIENCING DISRUPTION

One of the most misunderstood costs of acquiring a customer is trying to decouple the customer from an existing relationship. The friction is greater than it appears. Bonds can run deep, sometimes for tens of years, and no matter how superior Q2, the customer won't leave their supplier. In fact, your presence can have the opposite effect. Rather than weaken the relationship, it can galvanize the bond as supplier and customer unite together to resist change.

When a business is under disruption, the foundation which underpins existing relationships is being rocked. The fractures can force customers to look for new ideas and suppliers.

SECTORS WITH FEW BARRIERS TO ENTRY

Businesses with few barriers to competitors lack defenses. This variant is more likely to adopt new ideas as a matter of survival. Their competitive advantage stems from being nimble and able to change quickly. The variants change not because they want to be seen to innovate, but because they have no choice but to innovate. Change is a matter of survival.

66 Hey Sally, we know when you will buy.

Thin slicing ratchets up a notch when you include a data point called buying trigger. A misconception among many startup founders is as soon as a customer is aware they have a problem, they are in the market to solve the problem by buying a product.

The truth is they don't. There is a lag between awareness and action. A customer profile may experience a problem, but the customer is not in the market to solve the problem, all the time.

The reality is customers are trying to solve many problems, and the problem you are solving is in a queue with half a dozen others. Visualize a stack. Stacked upon one another are different problems. Sandwiched somewhere in that stack that towers one meter high is a problem you are trying to solve. In this respect, a startup is in competition not with other competitors, but in competition with a stack of other problems.

The buying trigger and trigger date are important data points to collect on a customer during prospecting. When you are not able to make an immediate sale, ask the question,

66 When is a good time to get back in touch?

This question is really asking "When do you think your company will put the job out to tender?"

It is a subtle way to tease out the trigger date. Knowing the trigger date is like revenue in the bank, because you know the precise date the buying decision will begin.

A customer profile may have a large ticket sale price or a large market size, but the customer profile is less valuable if the customer only makes a single buying decision annually. For example, a parent may be aware their children lose canteen money during school. This is a problem worth fixing. However, the parent is in no hurry to solve the problem until the kids return to school after the holidays. Awareness exists today, but action to solve the problem won't start until a future date.

C-Level employees from enterprise companies invite suppliers to tender on solving a problem. The tender is a procurement process many large entities must follow in order to appear equitable and unbiased. Irrespective of how acute the problem – how much money the enterprise customer is losing today – an enterprise decision-maker is compelled to follow a tender process. Dialogue to solve a problem will not commence until a tender date is set.

When do you suppose the best time to contact a mobile phone user about purchasing a new plan? Answer: when their contract expires. A telco that knows the date a customer's plan expires knows the buying trigger and trigger date. These are important data points. They know exactly when to pitch the customer an offer and make a sale. No matter how much grief the customer may endure during the 24 months leading up to the expiry, they may be reticent to solve the problem because of the cost of breaking a contract. The trigger date is the moment the sale will happen.

In the salon example, the chat agent knows Sally's buying trigger. The buying trigger is the new financial year. It is easiest for Sally to switch in the new year because transactions from the previous financial year do not have to be migrated. Only opening balances need to be brought forward.

Not only do we know the buying trigger, but we can predict the trigger date. Because all businesses in Australia share the same year-end date, we know the day Sally will close the books on the previous year.

We know when Sally will buy before Sally knows when she will buy.

Apart from calendar dates, triggers can occur at a particular hour of the day or day of the week. Sundays are notably a day of rest, and consumers are susceptible to making a buying decision because they have time. Small business owners put off making buying decisions until after 7pm because during daylight hours they are busy serving customers. Holidays, which were once a forbidden time of the year to contact customers, are now a feeding frenzy. Mobile phones have turned holiday periods from a dead zone into a time when consumers make high involvement decisions like the purchase of a car or a house.

The weather each day can affect buying triggers. In the U.K., we notice on warmer days customers entered fewer buying decisions. On warm days customers were preoccupied with spending time outdoors and less time in front of their computer.

Some buying triggers are easier to predict than others. Timing the arrival of an important decision-maker in town makes it difficult to forecast revenue. A change in legislation is easier to predict. Changes in legislation are often discussed in the public domain months before the changes take effect.

> TACTICS TO SNUFF OUT TRIGGER DATES

A tactic is to provide a service to help customers identify their trigger date. At Futurebooks, we designed a free service for startup business owners in Singapore to identify a variety of filing dates including annual general meeting, tax filing and tax installments. The service required minimal input from the customer and the report was valuable because it spelled out important dates.

Customers will yield a trigger date freely if it is in their interest to provide the date. Customers are grateful for the service because they avoid repeating the same mistakes in the following financial year. Futurebooks collected important intelligence on the trigger dates such as when tax was due to be paid to the Singapore Inland Revenue Authority.

In other situations customer profiles will not reveal their trigger date, even to close friends. An example is employees who are planning to leave their place of work and seek a new vocation.

Relying on the customer to tell you the trigger date is one tactic. The second source of intel may be found through desktop research.

When prospecting for new customers at Firestarter, a digital marketing agency I ran in the 2000s in Singapore, we monitored the number of new marketing hires made by enterprise companies over a period of 3 months. We watched all the major job posting sites and print publications, often clipping job ads and comparing the spend on each post.

New marketing hires are eager to stake their claim by throwing out existing agency relationships and initiating new projects. From the date when the hiring posts appeared, we calculated the trigger date forward three months. Had we begun knocking on the doors a month earlier or later, our pitch would have fallen on deaf ears.

> CREATING BUYING TRIGGERS

In rare situations, you may be able to artificially force the customer to prioritize a problem and bring forward a trigger date that may have been scheduled later. An event can trigger a customer profile to change priorities and decide to solve a problem you're trying to fix.

Normally this tactic creates urgency and simultaneously provides the trigger and the solution in one, in a time frame that is so short the customer has little time to evaluate alternatives. Promotions try to create artificial buying triggers like a limited time only offer or an offer to buy-out the remaining term on a phone contract. These efforts bring forward a trigger date that normally would exist in the future.

A direct approach incorporating fear can also work. Legal firms prepare in advance of changes announced by government. On the eve of the decision taking effect, they bombard their customer base with fear messages designed to capitalize on the change and trigger a buying decision. Fear, like opportunity, can hack a customer's trigger date.

> Q1 TAKEAWAYS

- 👉 identify three customer profiles you serve today and their respective customer goals and buying triggers

- 👉 thin-slice each customer profile into two or more variants who you serve today, tomorrow or never

- 👉 buying triggers and attitudes can be more important in predicting a sale than age or sex

- 👉 identify at least one profile you never serve

- ☆ new entrants: discover and capitalize on variants existing players have missed

- ★ existing players: you serve too many customer profiles and are remembered by none. Serve fewer customer profiles and concentrate on building endearing experiences in Q4

- ⏵ watch the 4Qs Insight, *Stop Wasting Time Serving Fake Customers*

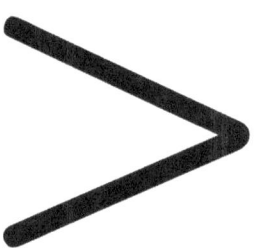

QUAD-RANT 2 WHAT WE SERVE

Quadrant 2 is all about the product fact sheet. A product fact sheet names the functions and limits of the product. This makes the product fact sheet like a television manual. This is the on button, this is the off button, this is how you change the channels and not only does it tell you all the functions of the television but it also gives you the limits. For example: do not operate in water. Knowing the television will not operate in water educates the customer that this is not an outdoor product. The customer learns as much about the product through limits as they do reading a list of functions.

So the product fact sheet is designed to be a public document. It is designed to help customer service make sure the right version of the product is being sold. I have seen situations where different people sell different versions of the product. In 2016 we conducted a friction test on a sector called cross border payments. When we interrogated the telephonist versus the online chat agent, we were sold a different version of the product. Getting on the same page about what we are selling, and naming limits improves the customer experience and reduces friction because we are tempering the customer's expectations early.

Normally the product fact sheet is updated each time the startup completes a development cycle or sprint. Each sprint ships new code to the public code base that customers enjoy immediately. Startups can complete sprints in less than a fortnight, effectively always shipping new product to the customer.

Because internet companies are always shipping, complacency in recording what is being shipped creeps in. Manufacturing companies adhere to strict guidelines that clearly list all the ingredients, instructions on how to use and assemble the product, and warning labels about misuse.

Strange as it may sound, one in two startups I talk to do not have a single point of view of what they sell. Partial manuals, no warning labels, assembly parts missing – meaning there was no point of view about

Q1 WHO WE SERVE	Q2 WHAT WE SERVE
Q3	Q4

exactly what was sold to the customer.

Trying to reach predictable sales without a clear definition of who you are selling to and what you are selling, is like trying to redeem a coupon advertising free beer tomorrow. It is a fantasy. For this reason, the product fact sheet now becomes our second quadrant.

While the customer profile is most often written by marketing people, the product fact sheet is written by the product people. If you ask marketing people to write the product fact sheet, expect a few extra features to get added and fluffy words to appear on the page.

The product fact sheet is a mutual understanding between the product and marketing teams about what is being sold today. It is a single viewpoint on what is the customer is buying. The product fact sheet lists every function and known limitation of the product. Each time the development team releases a sprint of code to the public, the product fact sheet is updated, a date appended and a new release number assigned. It is a way to know exactly what was sold on any day of the year.

The product fact sheet is a resource for many in the startup, not just the marketing and salespeople promoting the product to the public. Customer service relies on the product fact sheet to understand the full breadth of inquiries they may receive from customers, including a list of the features about to be shipped.

The CEO, to the customer service persons – every staff member and partner knows what functions ship with the product and only to discuss functions mentioned on the sheet.

If the product fact sheet performs one task well, it's to help a startup avoid the lethal mistake of future selling. The product factsheet is a discipline, a way to shield the company from making commitments to build features it cannot deliver. This is why the product manager, not sales and marketing, should write the product fact sheet and update the sheet with every subsequent release of the product.

> FUTURE-SELL IS EVIL

Future selling is when someone in the startup commits the company to build a feature tomorrow, in order to make a sale today. The startup falls foul of making the sale contingent on a feature that may not have been specified, costed or thoroughly tested with the code-base. Because the feature is unspecified, the precise date of the release is hard to predict, making the sale a moving target.

In the first year, the practice of future selling saves a lot of dev hours. You show wireframes and prototypes and gather the reaction of your audience. When you are a two-person company, the risk of future-sell is zero. You compromise no assets or staff because you have none. However, some founders never grow out of this practice and as the startup grows and hires staff, the risks associated with this practice become pronounced.

Future-sell introduces a second, more subtle infection. By allowing the customer to customize the order outside the product's normal parameters, you discipline the customer to believe they can shape the direction of product. For example, if you were the founder of a SaaS company, you risk becoming a business building bespoke software for individual customers. Once you position the company as a custom builder, the requests for custom build will not stop coming.

Founders and business owners are particularly prone to future sell because they have to sell product and the company vision. After a motivational speech on company vision by the founder, the founder takes a call from a customer wanting to buy the product. The founder, still flying at 40,000 feet, tells the customer more about the vision of the company and less about the product.

It is easy to confuse the company vision with the product, thereby future selling. The sale is the truth; it is where the rubber meets the road. Performing both can see visionary messages mix with sales messages, such that staff and customers think the product of the future is here now.

For this reason, many founders now include a "forward-looking statement" to try to indemnify them from accusations of future-sell.

I consulted to a startup where we future sold so often, the lines between what was fact and fiction become blurred. Each person in the company sold a different version of the product. Future sell to enough customers and your entire product roadmap is railroaded. You spend your days reporting to each customer on progress towards a future sale. With so many promises competing for resources, the company fails to deliver to all customers and you close no deals. No happy customers, no roadmap – just a big mess.

In some countries like Australia, future-sell is banned by law. If you decide to sell a financial product, you are not permitted to talk about the product until it is launched.

There's a third reason why I'm not hot on future-sell.

You can lose a sale. Take a look at this dialogue between a founder and a customer.

 Founder: We are opening a new office in Los Angeles next month.

Sally: Great. Let's talk then.

Founder: We are releasing a new feature next week.

Sally: Great. Let's talk then.

Founder: We are running a promotion tomorrow.

Sally: Great. Let's talk then.

When you future sell, you push the sale into the future. Future selling gives the customer a way of deferring the buying decision. Avoid future selling any news about the company – expansion plans, a new office, a new customer service persons who may be joining, a cool new campaign about to launch.

> SELL WHAT YOU HAVE IN THE WAREHOUSE

Let's rescript the founder.

 Founder: We have a monthly subscription plan which measures 10 meters tall and 5 meters wide. Available in two colors. We have one million units in the warehouse ready to ship today. Can I take your order?

A smart salesperson sells in the present tense. They keep the customer focused on the benefits the product has today. They formulate a pitch based on features the product ships, and close deals based on these features alone. They only talk about new features with customers, when the product manager updates the product fact sheet with new features.

Sell only what is printed on the product fact sheet and avoid customers who hold out or make a sale conditional on a future feature release. Or competitors who discover what is included in the next feature release, ahead of the release date.

> NAME LIMITS

The product fact sheet also needs to inform the customer of known limitations. In our television manual analogy, the manual is responsible for pointing out never to use the television in wet conditions or plug the television into an unsuitable power source. Limits improve a customer's expectation of what a product does and doesn't do.

Irrespective of the business model, there are limitations. In a tech startup, there are limits to the performance of the product and what the service staff can perform. Every product, no matter how perfect, has limits. It is important to name limits in the early game and avoid friction which can eventuate later when the customer's expectations are not met.

Price is a limit, especially when the product is not free or there is no work-around like a free trial. Along with the price, the product fact sheet can track other limits like the number of units sold in each pack. Not every product is available 24/7.

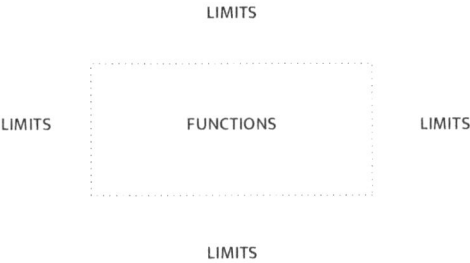

For example, a hair salon offering hair styling services may only be available from the hours of nine in the morning till five in the afternoon. Limits are experienced in a restaurant business, a consulting firm, and internet startups.

Restaurants serve what is on the menu. They have the ingredients readily available to create a set of dishes. Making limits known early manages customer expectations and reduces the chance you will inconvenience a customer. Placing trading times on

Google Maps tells customers when you are open before they leave their homes. Offering a menu when a customer arrives tells the customer what is available.

If you have ever been told your credit card is not accepted when trying to pay the bill, it is likely the restaurant didn't make limits known in the early game.

Remember: a customer learns as much from the list of functions as they do from the list of limits. The boundaries of expectations are defined by both.

Limits that are likely to become a friction point need attention. Identifying which limits are friction points and naming these limits early during communication gives the startup an opportunity to decide how to best couch a limit. Disguising a limit in the early game and revealing the limit in the endgame will only lose you the trust you built with the customer.

> WE GOT HACKED BY SALLY

Failing to name limits exposes your startup to a type of customer who hacks Quadrant 2 and 4.

When limits are not named, Sally could be conditioned to think your product is infinitely customizable. This inventive customer looks for every opportunity to create their own Quadrant 2 and 4. Sally, sensing there is no limit, writes the product fact sheet for you.

This financial liability is not felt when the startup has a single customer. However, at 100 customers, the problem is acute, with 100 customers each having their own way they want to work with you. This issue is similar to future-sell – customers are on different versions of the product.

Services like on-boarding, setup, customization, training and feasibility studies are vulnerable to this type of hack.

Once the customer has built a version of the product to suit themselves, any action on your part to adjust expectations is met with resistance. The only way to break the deadlock is to fire the customer.

> OFFER WORK-AROUNDS

There are times when customer support can prescribe a work-around. Work-arounds are a temporary measure designed to overcome friction until a more satisfactory result can be achieved. They permit a sale, without future-sell.

Even technology giants like Google with above USD 1BN market cap solve product limits with work-arounds.

Below is a real-life example of how Google uses a work-around to answer a customer's query about customizing a Google Doc:

 Jo S.: ...At this time, there is no way to have pages with different background and various colors in a single Docs document. The workaround is to create a separate document for the page that needs to be a different color.[3]

In the next example, Jo S. offers an add-on as a workaround.

 Jo S.: ...At this time it's not possible to rename the styles in Docs. However, there's an add-on called Paragraph Styles+ that allows you to create custom styles.[4]

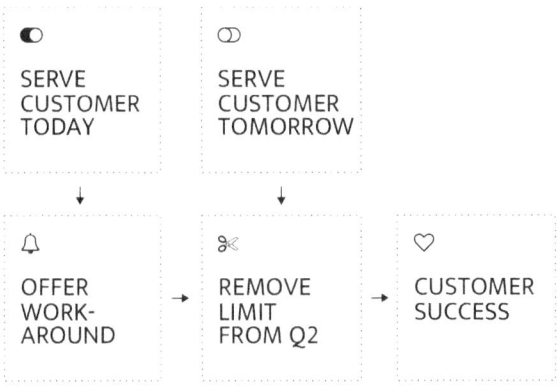

Of all four quadrants, friction in Quadrant 2 is the most difficult to eradicate because it involves re-engineering parts of the product. If your product is a service, it involves retraining staff who perform the service. If it is a physical product or technology, the improvement can take longer. It is back to prototyping before changes are made in production.

In every business, there is a time between when a friction point is assessed, to the time when the friction point is eliminated in Quadrant 2. During that time, companies offer work-arounds to customers.

InstaSave requires users to ensure sufficient funds are available on the pre-paid card, before attempting an

ATM cash withdrawal. Users unaccustomed to the concept of linked accounts may not appreciate there are two separately stored values and may complain an ATM withdrawal was declined unnecessarily.

This type of limitation is likely to be a friction point. A work-around would be to first transfer sufficient funds from the wallet to the pre-paid card, a task that be can done from the mobile app, before making the ATM withdrawal. Not raised early during communications with the customer, this limit can impede customer success.

In some situations, it may be better not to serve a customer profile from Quadrant 1 until the limit is overcome in Quadrant 2. The customer profile is deprioritized to a customer you serve tomorrow and the customer added to a waiting list.

Product roadmaps can be prioritized in terms of which limits should be eliminated first. The limits which produce the greatest friction should be dealt with first. The more features released that address limits, the less friction experienced by the customer.

In the Instasave example of the ATM withdrawal limit, a feature could be written which auto transfers funds from the wallet to the pre-paid card, whenever the card falls below a threshold. Solving limits in Quadrant 2 rather than naming a work-around is ultimately the best solution because it relies less on education and changing user behavior.

> DEFER CUSTOMIZATION

This situation particularly applies to enterprise customers who habitually take control of suppliers by rubber-stamping their product with customization. At some point, a customer from an organization much larger than yours will coerce, tempt or downright bully the startup into the customization corner. Customization is a variation of future-sell. It is value that may or may not occur in the future, sold today.

In such a situation you can try a tactic of deferring customization to a later date and perhaps the custom work can be fulfilled by a different organization. Here's how the script could read continuing from the earlier example:

 Sales agent: No. It doesn't appear our product supports this integration.

Thumbs through leaflet.

Sally: Can we have it?

Sales agent: What you see here is what we have today.

Sharing the sheet of paper.

Sales agent: However, if you sign up and become a customer today, it entitles you access to our special projects team.

Sally: How much will it cost?

> **Sales agent:** I am not able to estimate it. Special projects will look at your requirement and estimate the time and fee to implement this feature for you.
>
> **Sally:** OK.

Deferring customization keeps the salesperson routed in the present tense. It decouples a future sale from the sale in the present. This tactic buys the customer time to consider their request more carefully. Do they really need it and how would it work? With time, the requirement may evaporate either because the customer finds a suitable work-around or because their business changes, in which case you have saved your customer unnecessary development costs.

Notice the sales agent does not block the customer. They say yes and provide the customer with a way to satisfy their goal, while protecting the startup's product roadmap.

A customized product may not exist. Rather than block the customer and not offer customization, a product can be invented to serve this requirement. The dummy product is used as a means of putting the cost of customization into perspective, knowing the customer will never buy.

A footwear manufacturer selling protective clothing to motorcycle riders uses this strategy masterfully. Customers have realized they can get more miles from their boots if the boots could be resoled. The manufacturer advertises replacement soles, so during the buying decision, the customer believes they can get longevity from the purchase. It is not until the customer decides 12 months later to replace the soles, do they discover soles are priced almost the same as a new shoe. This footwear manufacturer has no intention of selling soles – the product is a dummy used to secure the sale of the core product.

> WHO THE HECK ARE TOM, DICK AND HARRY?

Working with partners has become fashionable. Startups can raise less capital and build fewer inhouse competencies by leveraging partners. For the same reason that you name limits, be upfront and tell the customer at the earliest convenience the partners with whom you work.

This analogy makes it clear. You've made a new friend, Lisa. Over a drink Lisa has got to know you and invited you to her Christmas party.

She has moved into a new home and redecorated. You arrive. Lisa answers the door. Rather than come alone, you've brought three friends. Lisa knows who you are, but has never laid eyes on your companions. There is an uncomfortable silence. Lisa is unnerved, confronted by new faces. For a moment your new friend considers whether she should permit you entry.

When bringing new faces to the party, it is customary to notify the host in advance, in case they have any objections.

The same applies during a sale. Sally has met you several times and invites you to pitch on her business. You're at the endgame – negotiating on terms of the sale. You decide to bring Tom, Dick and Harry, none of whom have ever met Sally. Tom is from the parent company to which the contracts will be made out. Dick and Harry are from two different consulting companies that provide maintenance and support.

Here comes the friction. The customer is distracted and not listening to the sales pitch. Turning over in the Sally's mind is:

> **Who the heck are Tom, Dick and Harry and what is their relationship with my supplier?**

Sally knows who you are, but has never met Tom or the others. You have inadvertently restarted the relationship at a time when the customer is ready to buy. All the trust you worked so hard to build in the early and middle game has evaporated. The entire sale has been rebooted and is now back in the early game.

Had you introduced Tom, Dick and Harry in the early

or middle game, the friction would be eliminated.

Another solution is to choose white label solutions when partnering with third parties. White labeling permits you to mask the identity of your partners, and use your logo and identity exclusively. By limiting the number of perceived partners, you have less credibility to establish in Quadrant 3.

There are exceptions to this rule. Where the name of the partner is well-known and respected, naming the partner has the effect of adding brand equity to your own brand. In 2017 Transferwise named Richard Branson on the company homepage as an investor in the company. Richard Branson needs no introduction. He is a well-known quantity and his association with Transferwise builds credibility.

Intel Inside® is another case where it pays to name the partner. PC manufacturers believe they are more likely to sell a laptop if they put a sticker on the product naming Intel as the provider of the CPU.

> AVOID SHARING THE PRODUCT ROADMAP

An extension of the product fact sheet is the product roadmap. The product roadmap is a projection of what and when features are coming. While it is common for part or the entire product fact sheet to make it into the public domain, the roadmap is confidential.

The product roadmap should be private and only be shared with select staff members and customers because it exposes the company to future-sell. If the roadmap ends up in the hands of customer, it becomes a promise and if it falls into the hands of a competitor, it becomes intel.

Neither situation is desirable. Both situations put the startup in a position where they are reporting to the customer.

> OFFER MORE THAN ONE PRODUCT

We have successfully eliminated friction caused by future-sell, customization and omitting to name limits. There is one final precaution we can take to help Quadrant 2 run frictionless. It involves augmenting the product.

Instead of offering a single product, and relying on every visitor to purchase that single product, augmented product widens the field and improves the odds every visitor will buy. Offering a single product makes each sale a zero or a one. You win or you lose. By augmenting the product you address the variants identified in Quadrant 1. You recognize the variants and each variant's attitude and buying trigger, and begin shaping a product to suit each.

Each customer not only buys the product now, but they repeat purchase, buying product A today and product B tomorrow. Instead of the salesforce relying exclusively on chasing new customers, you create a pipeline of predictable sales from existing customers the salesforce can chase.

Let's look at what tactics we can deploy if we augment product in Quadrant 2.

DOWN-SELL

Down-selling gives the customer a chance to experience the company at the lowest possible price. Offer a simple product to create this customer, like a $50 health check or a $10 ebook.

I prefer to down-sell a first-time customer more often than up-sell, especially in a startup where delivery of the service may be inconsistent. When you up-sell, you up the expectation. A small mistake can result in financial losses through refunds and being labeled disreputable. Selling a low price product keeps expectations low. If a mistake does happen, you are more likely to be forgiven.

Down-selling is one of the most effective ways to treat a price-sensitive variant. The reason is that price ceilings, unlike other kinds of buying criteria, are temporary, and can be moved once the customer experiences the company. Once you have earned the customer's trust, up-sell.

UP-SELL

When you offer a single product, it can be difficult to improve the lifetime value of the customer. With no up-sells available, the customer pays the same each time they interact with the company.

That may be financially acceptable, but for most startups I speak to they are trying to recoup as quickly the costs to acquire the customer. To achieve this financial goal, it is essential they up-sell because up-sells are one of the fastest ways to predictably grow revenue.

An up-sell is normally an extension of an existing product. It is premium or offers more usage. An example of an up-sell is offering an express experience. Pay more and jump the queue.

CROSS-SELL

A cross-sell is where a complementary product is offered. Amazon has this strategy down pat each time they publicize this alert on their website:

> Customers who bought ABC, also bought XYZ.

POST-SELL

Early in my career I ran a consulting company, Firestarter. We produced web applications and practiced a method we called post-sell. We never tried closing deals with a customer who did not perceive value in our services. No matter how high the quality of our work or attention to detail, experience taught us this customer profile would have a negative experience and write a poor review of our company, if we tried to serve them today. This became a customer we served tomorrow.

We had a few options. We could try educating this customer to change their thinking. This was expensive and success was not guaranteed. Instead, we decided to post-sell. We would encourage the customer to go to a competitor, who we knew would provide less service than we did, but at a reduced price.

In six months' time, we would re-approach the customer and invite them back. Invariably, the customer would have had a negative experience. Rather than absorb the cost and headache of educating the customer, we outsourced the education process to a competitor. Their expectations adjusted, they were ready to do business with us.

There is no use forcing a sale when the customer's expectations are mismatched. If your company has the vision and financial stability to think forward, post-selling is an effective strategy.

The CEO of Zappos, Tony Hsieh, in his book *Delivering Happiness,* tells a story where during a party with friends, he called Zappos pretending to order a pizza. Zappos is of course an e-commerce store selling shoes. However, Zappos has a policy to serve every customer, even if they don't offer a product. The telephonist who took Tony's call made inquiries and found pizza stores nearby his home. They didn't sell anything to Tony, but they did create a positive experience, making it easier for this person to become a customer of Zappos tomorrow.

> Q2 TAKEAWAYS

- 👍 name at least three limits which help manage customer expectations

- 👍 map one work-around for each limit and defer customization

- 👍 sell only what you have in the warehouse - future sell is evil

- 👍 understand equity built in Q2 is not defensible and is susceptible to being copied

- ☆ new entrants: introduce lightweight products to take down variants existing players have missed

- ★ existing players: build a second pipeline of customers you serve tomorrow by building a new feature set

- ▶ watch the 4Qs Insight, *Grow a consulting startup on the 4Qs*

QUAD-RANT 3 WHO WE ARE

In this chapter, we'd like you to welcome Tom to the stage. Tom is a part of your salesforce. He might even be the founder. We know Tom is not scalable. Tom goes on holiday, sometimes he's not well and other times we can't find him. If he is the founder, he's smooching investors. What happens then? Do we stop serving Sally because Tom's not around?

Rather than promise Sally she will interact with Tom all the time, we promise Sally she will have an opportunity to interact with a personality of a brand. Remember we don't always want salespeople serving customers. We want to automate much of our communication, and a brand identity is essential if we are ever going to free Tom from a sales role.

Sally still needs a personality to relate to and a brand identity is the perfect substitute for when Tom is not around. Customers like to buy from people they know because they value relationships.

Brands are a substitute for relationships with people, because having a real person at every customer interaction is not scalable.

The document we are most concerned with in this quadrant is the brand guideline. This document can be created internally if the founder or staff have design training. Or it can be created on behalf of the startup by a third party like a design agency.

The brand guideline describes the brand identity. Contained within a brand guideline are demonstrations of the clear space around the logo, the tone, use of colors, and what fonts are appropriate.

What should become apparent is that the logo is only part of the brand identity. The brand identity includes the visual language: color palette, choice of fonts, design motifs, photography, iconography and the tone of the language.

The treatment of the visual language and tone is as important as the treatment of the logo. These additional elements complete the brand identity, such

Q1 **WHO WE SERVE**	Q2 **WHAT WE SERVE**
Q3 **WHO WE ARE**	Q4

that even when the logo is not present in a customer interaction, brand recognition is achieved through use of color and fonts.

For startups a five-page brand guideline is sufficient. For a company in operation for 50 years or more, 100 pages are better. The more interactions a startup has with the customer, the more elements need consideration and the longer the brand guideline.

Come the next chapter we will begin designing customer interactions and placing those interactions in a timeline. Before we do, we will need a brand identity to help us consistently brand each of those interactions.

The minimum requirement for Quadrant 3 is consistent branding. A well-articulated brand guideline can help everyone achieve consistency by teaching staff, vendors and partners how to apply the brand in different customer interactions.

Apart from freeing the salesforce and appearing predictable, a brand can shape how your company is remembered. Friendly, safe, authoritative or carefree – these are a few personality traits conjured in the mind of a customer when they come into contact with a brand.

Being consistent in branding makes the buying decision for a customer frictionless. Instead of claiming you are safe and secure, the brand demonstrates these traits through tone.

If the brand fails to convey a tone or attitude, the words and pictures we wrap the sales system with later will lack impact. The brand will lack personality, and we'll need to call Tom and ask him to cut his vacation short and get back to the office.

No matter how you brand, you will be remembered for something. If the brand is disorganized, this becomes a cue to customers that the product and every aspect of the business are disorganized.

Each time the customer interacts with the brand, brand equity is built. Think of equity as a deposit account. The account builds each time the customer interacts with your company's brand. The more deposits made, the more likely they are to purchase.

> DELIVER A CONSISTENT BRAND IDENTITY

A consistent brand makes it easier for advertisers to attract customers to your doorstep. It provides the advertiser cut-through. A brand that is organized stands out.

To demonstrate this principle, imagine a disorganized space like a web page or an exhibition hall stacked wall to wall with exhibitors. The squares over the next page represent brands competing for attention.

Which squares grab your attention?

If you guessed the top left-hand corner you're right. The brand located top left-hand corner is immediately identifiable. An organized brand returns more value on every dollar spent attracting eyeballs to your front door.

We live in an unpredictable world. Each time I leave my home and I travel to work on foot, even though I take the same route every day, my experience is unpredictable. This is because traffic and weather conditions are never the same each day. Every day I need to worry about avoiding cars, potholes and inclement weather. I have to continuously think and calculate.

This is the same in the business and consumer world. Everything is unpredictable. Customers yearn for predictability and they are prepared to pay a premium

for it. Women are prepared to pay for an experience where they can sit in a hair salon, drink their favorite flavored tea, are greeted in a particular manner each time they arrive, know the kinds of products that will be used for the treatment and they know what time the blow dry will commence.

They are prepared to pay to get this predictability because as busy people, everything else in their lives is unpredictable.

When our lives are made predictable, we don't have to worry. We can relax and we can let others take control. The hair salon is taking out the worry because they have thought through the customer experience, so the customer doesn't have to do the thinking.

Customers can sit down, tune out, and enjoy the moment.

When a customer buys a product, they are buying more than Quadrant 2. They are also buying Quadrants 3 and 4; that is, they are buying your brand and an experience.

If you can brand every customer interaction consistently, you're making the customer believe that Quadrant 2 will be predictable. Well before the customer has experienced the product, the customer is forming an opinion that the product is quality. If the packaging is predictable, so must be the product.

This explains why some startups which excel in

Quadrant 3 are more successful than competitors that excel in Quadrant 2. In my experience, tech-led founders spend inordinate amounts of time perfecting Quadrant 2, and completely under-develop Quadrants 3 and 4.

Consciously or not, they are throwing Quadrant 2 at the customer and saying,

> Here's the product – make of it what you will

Two rival food manufacturers process and sell almonds. One manufacturer leaves the almonds on the shelf in buckets. There is no packaging and the user is invited to scoop the desired quantity of almonds into a bag. The second manufacturer has carefully measured out the quantity of almonds a consumer needs, packaged the almonds in an airtight tin and printed a brand on the tin plus all benefits of consuming the product.

Of the two, which manufacturer has commoditized their product and neglected Quadrant 3? Many startups make this mistake and overlook a bias – customers base the quality of Quadrant 2 on the packaging.

Consistently branding each customer interaction is important because it builds cues before customers buy the product from Quadrant 2: that we are a predictable organization and therefore the product they're buying is going to be of quality.

Founders make a second mistake in thinking that in order to increase price, they must spend more money on improving Quadrant 2, when in fact the answer to a price rise rests in Quadrants 3 and 4. No matter how good Quadrant 2, the customer won't know how good the product is until after they have bought. If Quadrant 3 is in disarray, the customer will expect the product is lower quality, and therefore, expects to pay a lower price.

If you believe first impressions count, then you believe investment in Quadrant 3 counts. Customers size up a product well before they read and compare the product features.

This is particularly important when you don't offer a free trial. Offering a free trial alleviates the pressure on Quadrant 3 by placing less emphasis on the packaging because the product can be trialed before purchase.

> ARE YOU A QUADRANT 2 FANATIC?

Technical founders I have observed are more likely to become Quadrant 2 fanatics. This is a founder who guards Quadrant 2 vehemently. No education materials pertaining to Quadrant 2 can be put in the public domain, so educating customers on features and limits is difficult. They firmly believe that if a competitor gets hold of their product fact sheet, the product will be recreated and up on the shelves in a matter of weeks, and they will automatically be out of business.

It's true. Quadrant 2 is difficult to defend against copycats. However, hiding Quadrant 2 is not the answer. The answer rests in Quadrants 3 and 4.

Two companies can offer identical products. The startup that can talk about Quadrant 2 in a different way using shared beliefs from Quadrant 3, or can create a unique experience in Quadrant 4, will sell more units because the customer thinks the products are different, even though they may be identical.

Insurance companies bank on Quadrants 3 and 4. Their customers seldom experience Quadrant 2, i.e., an insurance claim. So a customer's entire experience rests upon shared beliefs and how easy it is to sign up and make a payment. Because the customer is unlikely to come into contact with Quadrant 2, Quadrants 3 and 4 are everything.

In fact, in later chapters, you will discover Quadrants 3 and 4 are much more defensible than Quadrant 2.

Sales-led founders are more likely to be Quadrant 3 fanatics. They future sell in Quadrant 2 and prop up lack of product delivery by driving shared beliefs in

Quadrant 3 and creating superior experiences in Quadrant 4. It is not uncommon for them to sell three or four versions of the product, because they ignore Quadrant 2 and remind everyone that only shared beliefs matter.

Take 20 seconds to conduct this self-diagnosis.

	Yes / No
Spend 80 percent of my day or more on the product	
Have not planned what comes before or after the product	
Never held a sales job for more than 12 months	
Haven't had a voice call with a customer in the last 72 hours	
Believe you can raise prices if you improve the product	

If you answered yes to three or more of questions, chances are you qualify as a Quadrant 2 fanatic. It's time to reduce friction and start investing in Q3 and Q4.

☁ For more self-assessment tools visit runfrictionless.com.

> SHARING BELIEFS GIVES COMPETITORS A BAD DAY

Brand consistency is the minimum requirement of Quadrant 3. However, if you'd like to give your competitors a bad day, begin sharing beliefs with your customers. Sharing beliefs goes much deeper and stems from why a founder started the company.

Sharing beliefs give the customer a feeling of belonging. A shared belief gives a brand a reason to exist. The brand stands for a higher purpose other than to make money for shareholders.

It is true — customers from Quadrant 1 buy from Quadrant 2. Customers try to make a rational buying decision by comparing the features, limits, and work-arounds of various brands. However, Quadrant 3 disrupts the rational buying process by making it difficult to compare apples with apples.

Customers may decide to buy your product over a competing product because they like the direction the company is taking. They are prepared to pay more, or settle for less, because "these guys get me." When Quadrants 1 and 2 are parity, Quadrant 3 can be the opportunity to differentiate.

Here's what it sounds like when a customer shares your belief:

> **OMG. I've been telling people this for years. Finally, someone has listened to me and built this product.**

Do you hear their gratitude? They feel like you personally listened to them. They feel like they belong.

Sharing beliefs sets in motion a set of irrational buying forces that are near impossible for a competitor to mimic. The irrational buying force is so strong, that even when sales, product and operations people are screwing up, customers keep buying because they believe in the brand.

No matter how much product from Q2 you throw at the customer, customers are unlikely to buy unless they identify with the problem and direction a company is taking to solve the problem in Q3. Customers buy because they share beliefs and continue to buy until such time as the equity in Q3 has dried up. Quadrant 3 buys a company time to get the second and fourth quadrants back on track.

Once you begin sharing beliefs, share your belief with as many people as possible. Sharing beliefs can be promoted through the name of the company, its tagline, or in the value propositions. Here is how a few internet startups share their beliefs:

> Evernote. Remember everything.

> Slack. Be less busy.

> Xero. Beautiful accounting.

Be careful. Establishing a brand identity is not an automatic ticket to sharing beliefs. A founder could approach a well-known branding company, pay to have a well-defined brand identity created, and still not achieve shared beliefs. The brand identity may be augmented and have all the right cues, but an identity alone does not share beliefs.

Stronger than the brand identity is what the logo stands for, i.e., the beliefs behind the logo.

> ☁ If you are finding it difficult to identify your company's beliefs, this online quiz can help. It takes less than five minutes to complete and will give you a steer on shared beliefs.

> BELIEFS ARE INSIDE-OUT

It is easy to confuse a belief with a shared belief. We can mistakenly assume beliefs we hold in our hearts are shared among those around us. As early as possible you want to share and test your beliefs from Quadrant 3. You want to diagnose if your belief is shared by one person or many.

Anybody can have a belief, vision, or mission statement. The value is whether your staff, shareholders, and customers *share* your belief, vision, or mission statement.

Shared beliefs are not insincere words created by an advertising agency and plastered on billboards. They are real and they are shared between the founder, staff and the customer.

Sharing beliefs will gather people to your cause. Customers, staff and shareholders will stand with you, talk and share the belief as though it was theirs. Because it *is* theirs. You have struck shared beliefs. If your belief is not shared, you will appear to be a crazy person standing in a forest, shouting where no one can hear your voice.

The person who speaks a belief that is shared will gather followers and be recognized as a leader. That's why shared beliefs are not easy to create nor for a competitor to copy. Quadrant 3 is defensible because shared beliefs are inside-out. Shared beliefs start with the founder, infect shareholders, and staff, before attracting customers.

Have you ever worked in an organization where it's customers and staff does not share your beliefs? Tony Hsieh, in his book *Delivering Happiness,* tells a story about why he sold his first business to Microsoft. Tony describes how he hated coming to the office each day because he was surrounded by staff and customers who did not share his beliefs.

While Tony did well financially his motivation for selling was to divest himself of a company without beliefs. In his own words:

> I dreaded going to work. I was the co-founder ... and yet the company was no longer a place I wanted to be at.

If you don't begin thinking and sharing your belief today, in two or three years you will experience internal friction. If people have different beliefs they will see your improvements as a threat to their belief and resist change.

Only by divesting yourself of the business or firing staff and customers and attracting new people will you overcome the internal friction.

> TESLA CRUSHES THE QUADRANT TWO FANATICS

In 2020 Tesla launched the Cybertruck. During the live product demonstration, the glass on the passenger door shattered. In a sense, Elon's product demo failed. The Quadrant 2 fanatics (disguised as automotive journalists) wrote that the Cybertruck was ill-conceived and doomed to fail.

Customers disagreed. At the close of business the following day, Tesla posted a press release claiming they had received over a hundred thousand orders of the truck[5].

What we witnessed that day was how powerful it is when an organization can tap the irrational buying forces of shared beliefs. Tesla's customers didn't care whether the glass broke or not. They know all companies have bad product days. They buy Tesla because they believe in the direction the organization is taking.

Every company, including your business, is going to have bad Quadrant 2 days. The difference is whether your customers will forgive you or crucify you.

> ❝ 150,000 orders taken for the Cybertruck.

> SHARED BELIEFS ARE NOT SHARED BY EVERYONE

When a founder exits a startup, so can shared beliefs. Imagine Sally has contacted your business, which you recently acquired. Sally has dealt with the previous owners on numerous occasions and expects to be able order and receive the same products, just as she has done in the past.

However, you do not empathize with Sally. You have no interest in serving her. By ignoring Sally, you hope Sally and those like her will go away.

Shared beliefs lock in some customer profiles and lock-out others. The decision to adopt a shared belief impacts who you serve in Quadrant 1.

JustPayroll set about creating the most compliant payroll application ever seen in the Philippines. This won them a large contract with the Philippines government. However, the shared belief simultaneously locked out a customer profile who wanted to be able to manipulate exported payslips.

Building this feature would contradict the company's shared beliefs. They refused to build this feature and the customer profile was labeled a customer they would never serve.

Before the internet arrived, it was possible for a brand to share beliefs discreetly with multiple customer profiles. Media channels were disparate and the chances of a company being discovered as inconsistent were next to nil. Today, social media equalizes any disparity by allowing different customer profiles to share their experience in a commonplace. Companies must take a position in Q3 and be prepared to hold it for the long term, despite the impact the decision will make on Quadrant 1.

This equalization effect on sharing beliefs is felt particularly by nightclub owners. Nightclubs are a business where customers meet other customers, so it is not possible to create discreet shared beliefs with different customer profiles. For a nightclub owner, the customer is a community and part of Quadrant 2. Patrons go to a club to meet like-minded people. The wrong profiles at the club dilute Quadrant 2.

Nightclubs refuse entry to customer profiles they don't serve, even when their floor space is under utilized. If they did permit entry, the risk is they would screw up a bunch of quadrants.

A > The wrong profile orders items not available on the menu.

B > The wrong profile suggests changes to the decor of which other patrons would not approve.

C > Customers who share beliefs retaliate.

In short, the profile has bought nothing, offered irrelevant intelligence and disrupted customer profiles the club does serve.

Where startups go wrong is when they lack the conviction to stick with shared beliefs. I see startups begin with a shared belief, and 12 months later, abandon the belief. Perhaps they abandon the belief because they got scared. It takes courage to turn away business.

Companies justify the decision to serve anyone because as long as product is selling, they feel safe. They don't care who buys the product or why they buy it. They don't realize how vulnerable they are to competitors mounting assaults on Quadrant 3.

> MAKING PROFIT AIN'T A SHARED BELIEF

If your sole purpose is to make a profit, as a founder you will never be free of a sales role. Here's why.

There will be days when the firm is not winning, not selling and not making money. On those days, what will be your motivation to come to the office? A higher purpose will give you the motivation to work even when profit is not made.

Another problem: not everyone is sharing in the profit. Often it is the directors and shareholders who hold the lion's share of the profit. Those profiles who are not sharing the profit need a higher purpose, otherwise profit-making will remain a belief held by few, and not a shared belief.

I regularly visit one of my favorite Honda dealerships. I noticed each time I visited one particular man who seemed to do all the serving. I turned to him on one of my visits and commented:

 Mr C: You're a shareholder in this business, aren't you?

Salesperson: Yes I am.

It was plain as day. He was selling out of a belief of making profit. The remaining staff, unlikely to be part of the profit-sharing, didn't share the belief. None had an urgent desire to serve the customer.

This wasn't a startup. This was a 20-year-old company that hadn't seen that if they were going to free the founder from a sales role, they must have a higher purpose than to clear inventory.

Profit should be a bi-product, not a belief. If the founder keeps telling staff to sell because we need to make revenue, they will never free themselves from a sales role.

> INTERMEDIARIES AND PARTNERS CAN DILUTE SHARED BELIEFS

In Quadrant 1 we identified a customer profile called "customers you serve through." These intermediaries have an existing install base of customers we can reach. However, has the intermediary created a 4Qs picture of its business? If the intermediary and your startup do not share beliefs, it is likely the intermediary will introduce friction.

A >   Do they serve the right customer profile?

B >   Will they consider the effect that bundling your product with other brands will have on your company's shared beliefs?

C >   Do they understand your shared beliefs, and are they willing to emulate them when interacting with their customer?

D >   Will they know the product fact sheet as well as your company, and avoid making the mistake of selling different versions of the product to different customers?

When founders make a decision to serve through, the decision is often one of product. These decision-makers are often Quadrant 2 fanatics who believe as long as the product is out there in as many places as possible, we are selling. And if we are selling, we are making money.

In a biography written by Walter Isaacson titled *Steve Jobs*, Walter explains that Jobs didn't:

> ...want an iMac sitting on a shelf between a Dell and Compaq. Unless we could find a way to get our message to customers at the store, we were screwed.[6]

Jobs' big concern was how resellers were diluting shared beliefs with customers. The only part of the process Apple didn't control was the instore buying experience. The specialty stores which once formed a large customer profile for Apple's sell-through strategy were closing and being replaced by large megastores.

The megastores were staffed by people with no Apple product knowledge and only a rudimentary appreciation of Apple's shared beliefs. These megastores had an overriding belief: sell the cheapest product and the product that yields the most margins. Apple was more expensive than competing lines, so this wasn't going to work.

In late 1999 Jobs began designing the first Apple retail store headed by Ron Johnson. Johnson asked Jobs if the Apple brand was bigger than GAP? Jobs replied, "Yes". So Johnson said the Apple store would be larger, to reflect the magnitude of the Apple brand.

Like Apple's shared beliefs of minimalism, the store design would need to be airy and creative. The store would become the most powerful physical expression of the brand. The customer interactions which took place under the roof of the stores would reinforce shared beliefs. The Apple stores would become not just another customer interaction, but a key interaction.

When the board of Apple saw the prototype store Jobs and his team built in an old rented warehouse, they unanimously supported the rollout of Apple stores as essential to reinforcing share beliefs among customers and staff. They realized the megastores would commoditize their business by driving down the company's value in Quadrants 3 and 4.

Marketplaces like Ebay.com are rather similar to megastores. Marketplaces try to create a level playing field between retailers by delivering Quadrants 3 and 4 on behalf of the retailers.

It is no surprise retailers complain marketplaces encourage price wars. With Quadrants 3 and 4 flattened, they have fewer advantages.

> THE RELATIONSHIP BETWEEN VALUES AND BELIEFS

Once you have a belief, you can figure out your values. Values drive-home the belief and make sure the belief is shared. Values help operationalize a belief and make the belief easy to apply to everyday situations.

Now, that doesn't mean you draft a dozen values. In truth, you can probably afford to only operationalize two or three values. Here's why.

Firstly, include only values that return value to a profile in Quadrant 1. Remember, we don't serve everyone and therefore, we don't need to empathize with everyone.

Secondly, for each value you espouse, you need one interaction from Quadrant 4 to demonstrate that specific value. The company must be prepared to invest dollars. Without an investment in Quadrant 4, organizations have vanity values.

Vanity values add friction because they are not actioned. They take up precious space where other words and pictures could appear. Worse, organizations with vanity values are deceiving their staff, shareholders and customers.

An example of this deception is the story of the CEO who wanted his retail business to become agile. This CEO recently learned how companies were becoming agile. He became convinced if other companies were agile, his business needed to be agile.

66 Call the public relations company! We are going agile.

The CEO spent the next six months convincing prospects and customers his organization was agile. While people outside the business believed him, the CEO did not spend time discussing this value inside the organization.

Here are a few problems that ensued.

Firstly, the organization did not reward staff for transforming Quadrant 4. Rather, it penalized them. If your idea failed, you failed with it.

Secondly, while the CEO made a big splash outside the company, he spent no time sharing his value inside the company. Staff found it difficult to connect how agile translated to a benefit to customers, and as such, largely ignored it.

Later when customers contacted the organization, they discovered nothing had changed. Piercing the organization's marketing veneer, customers found themselves face-to-face with the same processes and cultures from before. They had been served a vanity value and had been deceived.

> Q3 TAKEAWAYS

- 👉 equity from Q3 is far more defensible than equity from Q2
- 👉 if packaging in Q3 is superior the customer will decide Q2 must be superior
- 👉 tap Q3's irrational buying forces that eclipse the rational buying forces found in Q2
- 👉 you can have a belief but it has no value if it is not shared by others
- 👉 shared beliefs lock in some customer profiles and lockout others impacting who you serve in Q1
- ☆ new entrants: identify Q2 fanatics and take them down with shared beliefs and pricing increases
- ★ existing players: capture more market share by repositioning the brand to appeal to a greater number of customer profiles
- ▶ watch the 4Qs Insight, *Frictionless customer experience*

QUADRANT 4 HOW WE SERVE

We have tackled three of the four quadrants. Quadrant 1 identifies customer profiles. In Quadrant 2, we work out what we serve customers. The third quadrant covers brand consistency and sharing beliefs. With these three quadrants behind us, we arrive at Quadrant 4, how we serve.

Quadrant 4 is the founder's dream. What makes the fourth quadrant exciting to design is beginning with a blank canvas. What does it feel like to become a customer of your startup? Is it colorful, delightful, or is it bloody painful? What's going to make the experience memorable for the customer and how will their experience with your startup be different from others?

Unlike Quadrants 1, 2 and 3, Quadrant 4 is free of limits. Quadrant 1 limits you to serve a select customer profile. Quadrant 2 limits you to the boundaries of the product. Quadrant 3 limits the number of customers who share our beliefs.

Not Quadrant 4. Quadrant 4 is limitless. It demands you put your creativity to use. You can create an experience you would like to have and the one you want your customer to have.

When it comes to Quadrant 4, the competition is wider than the industry you serve. The competition is every consumer and business interaction the customer has had in the last 12 months. That's the bar. So you can borrow inspiration from an amazing holiday you took at Disney Tokyo or from an electronic gadget you bought from Apple and unboxed.

With fresh eyes, founders can look at an industry and see new ways to address a customer who may not have been attracted to buy earlier, unlocking new customer profiles and new revenue. Based on the experience created in Q4, it is not uncommon to reverse-engineer parts of Quadrants 1, 2 and 3.

The picture we have built up in each of the previous three quadrants is essential to creating a memorable experience in Quadrant 4.

Q1 **WHO WE SERVE**	Q2 **WHAT WE SERVE**
Q3 **WHO WE ARE**	Q4 **HOW WE SERVE**

Had we disregarded Quadrants 1 through 3, the interactions we would design in Quadrant 4 would be hollow. The interactions would lack purpose and appear to the customer as thrown together.

Q4 can be thought of as the minimum number of customer interactions required to make a customer. A customer interaction occurs each time the startup comes in contact with the customer. These are the moments when the customer experiences the startup. One startup may require five value propositions, 30 email scripts, three PDF documents, one video, one live chat and one telephone call, before a customer is created.

Interactions are plotted in sequence according to when the interaction will take place. Each interaction has a channel where the interaction will take place, for example, an online chat. By playing with these variables such as sequence, timing, and channel, founders can create unique and memorable experiences.

Sally is faced with making a buying decision. She is considering one of two insurance products. The two insurance products are priced similarly, with similar feature sets. Stood side by side it's hard to tell the difference. Both share a similar Quadrant 2. However, Product A accomplishes Sally's goal in under 10 interactions. It takes five minutes to apply for a quote online, provides a clear message the form was submitted and sends SMS updates to Sally.

Sally completes the entire experience from her mobile phone.

Product B has twice the number of customer interactions and takes twice as long to complete because it is full of friction points. The starting point to the journey is not clear and requires Sally to download and fill in a PDF. Sally has to make a special trip to her friend's place as she doesn't have a printer at home. After submitting the document, Sally is not sure if her request was received or acted upon.

Recall times when you have bought a product and had a good experience. It is the experience that stuck and kept you coming back and buying, and telling friends.

Like Q3, Q4 is a cue to how great or pitiful Q2 will play out. Q4 and Q3 work together to leverage Sally's desire for a predictable customer experience. At the hair salon, Q3 ensures the decor, the color of the fresh flowers placed on the credenza, are consistent with the brand identity. Q4 sees Sally is served a cup of her preferred tea and that her favorite products are used during the treatment.

The document best to track Q4 is a customer flow, which can be presented as a flow diagram in any type of presentation software. The customer flow has a few names which all mean much the same – customer map, customer journey, a sales funnel or sales process.

> THE EARLY, MIDDLE + ENDGAME

Broadly, every customer interaction can be grouped in either the early, middle or endgame. The early, middle and endgame is a cute and memorable way of understanding the customer's buying decision. The three stages can be referred to as awareness, evaluation and purchase.

We use this classification to help the salesforce understand where a customer is snagged and what action to take to nudge the customer forward. Placing customers into stages helps the salesforce understand what to do next.

It is commendable if you have 20 prospect customers. It's grand if you know you have 15 in the middle game, two in the endgame and three that just popped in before lunch into the early game. Understand the precise location of each customer in a system and you can forecast financials and customer conversion rates.

The definition of the early, middle and endgame will differ from startup to startup. Generally, early game handles first-time interactions with a customer – customers who complete an online web form, call in via phone, decide to live chat, or drop an invitation to talk on Twitter.

The middle game is a gestation period, a time when the customer is evaluating competitors, including the option of "sticking with the status quo." The middle game, as the word suggests, sits in the middle between the early and the endgame, and normally contains the largest number of customer interactions.

The endgame is where the customer has shortlisted suppliers and is preparing to close out their buying decision.

This does not include people who come to your site and join your newsletter. Newsletter subscribers are pre-early game. They have not signaled an intention to purchase – rather they want to get to know you.

> SERVE MORE WITH LESS

Mapping every customer interaction in an early, middle and endgame is important because it teaches you the drop-off rates between the early game, early to middle, and middle to the end. For example, if you have 20 customers who enter the early game, and if the drop-off rate is 50 percent in the middle game, and 20 percent in the endgame, customer acquisition figures look like this.

	early	middle	end
drop-off	-	50%	20%
customers	20	10	8

By understanding the early, middle and endgame, and the associated drop-off rates, you can quickly grow your company.

By turning a few dials, you can make a big impact on the bottom line. Let's say you improve the value propositions in the early game. The change results in a decline in drop-offs from 50 percent to 40 percent in the middle game. Without making big changes, and just turning a few dials, the company increased the number of leads in the endgame from eight to 10, an increase of 25 percent. A staggering number for a small change. You didn't redesign the product, you didn't change your sales strategy.

	early	middle	end
drop-off	-	40%	20%
customers	20	12	10

The endgame is expensive because this is where the majority of the salesforce's time is spent. So you want high rates of drop-off to occur in the early or middle game – that way, by the time a customer arrives in the endgame, the odds of closing a deal are high.

By qualifying customers at each stage of the buying decision, you increase the chances that the salesforce are focusing on real deals, and not fumbling with customers who never intend to buy.

> SERVE CUSTOMERS FASTER

E-commerce in late 1990s promised customers a better customer experience than traditional retail. While online shopping did allow a customer to shop all hours of the day, buying online was not ideal. Slow internet connection, heavy page sizes, long sign up forms for first-time buyers and poorly categorized products meant the customers spent more time online than if they bought an equivalent product in-store. Online shopping had more friction than traditional retail shopping.

E-commerce has improved dramatically, due to faster internet connections, smartphones with fast processors, and more intuitive buying experiences. Compared to buying online, in-store purchases today feel like shopping in slow motion.

E-commerce has achieved the minimum expectation of a customer flow – it's faster. Not fast, faster.

If you are unable to create a memorable experience in Quadrant 4, then at least make the experience fast. Serving the customer first is the minimum requirement for Quadrant 4. Startups can win business simply because they serve the customer first, not because they have a better product.

Think about achieving the customer's goal as a race. The starting gun can be heard the moment a customer makes contact in the early game. The first startup to get the customer to the endgame wins the sale. The race is one to satisfy the customer's goal, either before a competitor does, or before the customer's goal expires.

A customer may appropriate one hour, one day or one year to making a buying decision, depending whether they classify the decision as low or high involvement. A low involvement decision has a short duration. A low involvement decision requires acute attention to response time because the buying decision can be over in a few minutes.

High involvement decisions are longer in duration and have many times more interactions, meaning more points where the experience can fail. High involvement decisions are like a marathon. Startups fail to close enterprise sales not because their product is inferior, but because they cannot manage a large number of interactions. It is not uncommon for the number of customer interactions to number between 20 and 30 interactions.

Buying decision	Customer expiry	Customer interactions
Low involvement	one hour	5
High involvement	one year	24

Emergency services talk about response time. History shows if emergency services arrive at an accident a few minutes quicker they can change the outcome dramatically for victims of a road accident.

Response time is an easy dimension to win a customer. If you serve a customer before your competition does, the customer will interpret this as cue to the quality of Quadrant 2.

If Quadrant 4 is superior, the customer will decide Quadrant 2 must be superior.

> **❝ Wow, if they are this quick serving me, imagine how good the product will be.**

This explains why companies with inferior products make sales over companies with superior products. They win based on speed.

It astounds me how slow businesses are to responding to customers, particularly in the early game where every second is precious. They are too placid, allowing the customer to cool and their goal to expire. If you're not shoveling from the early to the middle game within a few hours, you're allowing customers to drop off. If you are not moving your customer from the early to the middle, and from the middle to the end game, your competitors will.

In the U.K. during 2016, we conducted a friction test on visa immigration service providers. A request for visa services was sent to 30 licensed immigration providers. Here were the results:

A >   50 percent of agencies contacted didn't acknowledge they received the request in the first hour.

B >   80 percent overall failed to interact in less than 24 hours.

That means that 80 percent of businesses didn't try to move the customer from the early to the middle game. This friction test demonstrates how a new entrant can win business by not having a better Quadrant 2, but by being faster in Quadrant 4.

> BUILD TRUST AND SERVE: BOTH METRICS COUNT

In exchange for satisfying their goals, customers offer their trust. Trust allows a customer to feel at ease and be led and makes the sale economically viable for the startup. When customers don't trust you they will buck, complain and try to create their own customer flow. A company that fulfills the customer's goals simultaneously builds trust. This is because the customer's goal and their trust are correlated.

To close the customer in the endgame, the startup must have built trust in the early and middle game. Once the customer reaches the endgame, if their trust is peaking, the chances of closing a sale are high.

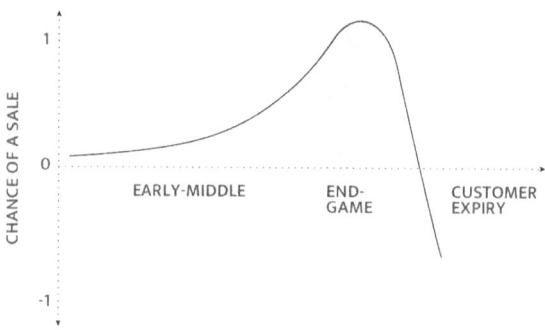

However, each hour that the startup tries to serve the customer after expiry, trust is inverted. That means Sally didn't buy, and equally Sally told her friends not to buy, creating a deficit. The deficit is not easy to spot. Startups might track whether a sale is lost or won, but don't track whether trust is lost or won.

Tom is in the business of retailing electric scooters. Tom has been pursuing Sally, hoping to close a sale. He is hopeful if he becomes buddies with Sally, Sally will become a customer.

 Tom: I did everything for Sally. I called her every few days. I even bought her lunch. Last week she stopped taking my calls. Now I hear Sally went with one of our competitors.

While Tom was busy "building a relationship" with Sally, someone else was busy helping Sally achieve her goal. Hearing Sally is going to a competitor, Tom retaliates. He begins leaving lots of messages and begging for the business. If Sally won't buy being his friend, surely pressure tactics will work.

It doesn't work. Sally is really annoyed with Tom. Sally hasn't bought from Tom and she never will. Over lunch with a friend, Sally tells her about the experience.

 Sally: Whatever you do, don't buy from Tom. He is a nightmare to deal with.

Customers don't want to talk. They want to get stuff done. They want to buy products to solve problems. A well designed sales system builds trust and increases the probability of a sale, simultaneously.

A well-designed customer flow gives a customer confidence. With each interaction, the customer feels like they are making progress towards achieving their goal. It signals you understand their goal and they can trust you to lead. When a customer surrenders and allows the startup to take control, the exercise is effortless for both the customer and the startup.

Tom's biggest mistake was having no sequence of how to create a customer. He made up the experience as he went along, writing fresh material every time he served a new customer.

A tell-tale sign that no experience has been designed is when you catch the salesforce writing lengthy bespoke email. When customer expiry is counting down, there isn't time to design a customer flow. The flow needs to be prepared in advance otherwise the interactions will be slow.

No matter how much effort the salesforce put into the middle and endgame, the time spent is of no value to the company or customer, if the customer's goal has expired. The window of opportunity never appears because trust was never significant and the customer's goal was only partially achieved.

> FEWER INTERACTIONS MAKE FOR LESS FRICTION

Make every interaction count. Every interaction must serve a purpose and help the customer get closer to their goal. Eliminate interactions that do not serve a purpose and bloat the flow. The fewer interactions you manage, the less friction.

During our discussion on Quadrant 3, I recounted how Steve Jobs wanted to open Apple stores to control the customer experience. Before Apple launched its first Apple retail store in 2001, they began with a prototype built in a warehouse. Steve was obsessed with driving down friction and questioned every customer interaction that took place in the store, removing purposeless interactions.

> " Steve gave us the exact, explicit recipe about how he wanted the check-out to work.[7]

I recently visited a Thai restaurant I dine at weekly and noticed that ordering, getting my meal and settling the bill had got easier. Previously they asked customers to post-pay for their meal. Many restaurants use a post-pay system shown below.

01	02	03
SEAT CUSTOMER	REQUEST A MENU	ORDER MEALS

04	05	06
REQUEST THE BILL	BILL PAYMENT	RECEIPT + CASH CHANGE

The problem with post-pay is it keeps the customers waiting at the table once they complete the meal. The wait time can be as long as 20 minutes. Their goal is to vacate and get to their next destination. Customers enjoy a wonderful meal, only to be kept waiting when trying to leave the restaurant.

The owners' solution to the problem was to switch from post-paid to pre-paid. Staff take the order and collect payment, before seating the guest. Instead of six interactions, pre-paid required only three as shown below. The entire bill collection was collapsed to a single interaction called payment, eliminating the need to request the bill and collect the receipt.

01	02	03
ORDER MEALS	PAYMENT	SEAT CUSTOMER

The benefits of pre-paid were felt instantaneously.

A > Customers could leave the restaurant as soon as their meals were finished.

B > Staff no longer shuttle back and forth from tables to the till. With less floor traffic, the space in the restaurant became more relaxed.

C > Tables could be cleared earlier increasing the capacity of the restaurant.

D > Less staff training was required because there were fewer interactions to manage.

E > Managing fewer interactions meant a greater chance of eliciting a positive review from a customer.

Hunt for alternative channels to deliver interactions competitors have overlooked.

> BOOK ONLINE, INSTEAD OF EMAILING

Appointment setting is a classic interaction that can spiral out of control. Sally would like to book a consultation over email to see a clinician. Here's how the interaction unfolds:

 Sally: I would like to book an appointment this week.

Agent: We have three times available. One on Tuesday, one on Wednesday and another on Friday.

Sally replies one day later.

Sally: I'll take the Tuesday appointment.

Agent: Sorry. That appointment is now taken. Can I suggest...

This interaction can be repeated several times before an appointment is reached. The agent tries to remedy the friction by telephoning Sally, committing a cardinal sin by making the interaction high touch.

A better way to overcome friction is installing a web-based, self-service booking application that allows Sally to see available times and make an immediate buying decision. Being a single interaction it has less opportunity for friction and less chance the customer will drop off.

We can overcome friction by rethinking the medium the interaction is delivered in. Instead of hosting an unstructured dialogue via email, we remove the dialogue completely and take an online booking.

Existing	New
Telephone booking	Online booking
Email reminder	SMS reminder
Print and sign	Online signature

> SIGN ONLINE, INSTEAD OF PRINTING

Verification is sometimes required by a company before they can do business with a customer. The customer has to prove their identity or financial position before they are eligible to buy. Verification can involve six or seven separate interactions including the customer printing documents, signing documents, scanning documents, attaching the scanned documents to email and finally sending the attachment.

Fintech startups are acutely aware of the friction imposed by verification because they know this interaction has a high drop-off rate.

Print and sign may look like a simple interaction. However, when you break it down, this interaction is brimming with friction. Let's see how Sally handles a verification to be eligible for a new credit card.

 Sally: Print the document.

Printer: Install printer driver.

Sally installs printer driver.

Sally: Print the darn document.

Printer: No paper.

Sally hastily loads paper.

Sally: Print the document you dummy!

Printer: Out of toner.

Sally loads new toner and crosses her fingers.

Sally: Print the document, please.

Printer: Paper jam.

See friction and drop-off mounting? While this is happening, the customer's goal is expiring. As a business owner, you cannot see this friction when it happens but you can anticipate it and experiment with new channels.

Here are a few ways we can augment verification (or remove it altogether).

A > Let's kill the printer, the scanner, and the pen to sign the document. In their place, we will put an online signature application that accepts electronic signatures.

B > Delay verification for as long as possible. By delaying verification, the customer can get on with their goal of creating an account or loading a transaction. Only at the time the customer decides to execute a transaction is verification required.

C > Lobby government to change legislation. Google made great strides lobbying government[8] to permit driverless cars. Similarly, governments are recognizing electronic signatures as legally binding.

D > Contract a partner to handle verification. Like Quadrant 2, Quadrant 4 can take advantage of partners. A partner may have designed a better customer experience, removing all the friction.

> TREAD CAREFULLY WHEN SWITCHING CHANNELS

Don't confuse communicating in another channel with switching channels.

Have you experienced a sales agent trying to move from an online chat to a telephone call? Or from a telephone call to an email? You are mid-conversation and the agent wants to change the channel. It disrupts the experience.

In 2018 we friction tested clinician practices in Sydney Australia. To test if clinics would block a customer in the middle game, the customer attempted to book a consultation over email. Each of the four clinicians contacted refused to take a booking to see an eye specialist unless the customer telephoned the clinic and made an appointment over the phone.

 Sally: I'd like to book an appointment to see the clinician either tomorrow or Friday.

Agent: I'm sorry, we cannot take your booking. Call this number now.

Clinical practices blocked the customer and insisted the customer talk on their terms. The clinic opens dialogue on email, but in the next customer interaction, insists the customer shifts to a telephone call. The salesforce has introduced friction. They risk restarting the buying decision or the customer dropping off. If a customer wants to use online chat to reach their goal, keep them in online chat. Don't insist they switch to another medium. This practice is a fast way to friction.

There are circumstances where asking the customer to deviate from their goal produces a better experience. For example, Sally wants a quotation to have a bookkeeper build her company's management accounts. Sally's goal is to get a quotation. Before providing what Sally wants, the accounting firm asks Sally to provide more information. By providing more details about her circumstance, the accountants can advise if Sally is seeking the right product, and advise her of a better solution.

This is a dangerous play, but it can pay off. First though, you will need to build trust. When a customer trusts you, they will allow you to lead them.

> NAILING THE KEY INTERACTIONS

Key interactions are turning points in the customer journey. They are the interactions that have the greatest impact on achieving the customer's goal. Key interactions occur when significant value is delivered to a customer, or an important decision is made that will triage the customer into the right customer flow.

There are no rules when key interactions take place, but in my experience, a key interaction normally marks the beginning of the middle and endgame.

In 2015 I conducted an experiment to see how influential key interactions were when eliciting positive reviews from a customer. I bought an apartment and decided I would start a business renting the space to holiday seekers. The apartment number was P601.

I spent a few months decking out P601, installing the kinds of gadgets my customer profile expected from Quadrant 2. We were focusing on the longstay family holiday seekers. These were groups of three to four people who would stay for a week or longer. I had custom paintings mounted on walls and a bespoke piece of European leather furniture positioned in the lounge room. I engaged the house manager of the apartment block to manage P601 and briefed their team on what we needed to achieve in Quadrant 4.

After a few months of operation, we gathered intelligence from feedback and problems customers encountered. We discovered we needed a maximum of 10 interactions before we could close a customer in the endgame. However, our business could be reduced to three key interactions.

If we made these three interactions flawless, we stood a 90 percent chance of a positive review.

The three interactions were:

A >   Collect the check-in/check-out times prior to arrival.

B >   Provide a guided tour of the apartment and amenities.

C >   Courtesy message three days post check-in.

Of all 10 interactions, we put 80 percent of our effort into three interactions. We spent hours talking about each of the three, collectively studying customer feedback and examining how we could go deeper into each.

After six months of operation, we became experts in these key interactions, splitting each into smaller interactions we could perfect.

Collecting check-in and out times was important in setting up a successful check-in. For customers who indicated they were arriving after 7pm, we post-sold their first night and encouraged this customer profile to stay a night near the airport at a hotel. This meant they arrived the following day having had sleep and we could perform a successful check-in.

The guided tour ensured the customer learned how to get maximum value from the amenities including how to use the sound system, reset the safety deposit box and operate the jacuzzi. Any limitations of the product were explained so customers didn't have to send unnecessary inquiries later.

The courtesy message three days post check-in was a safety net. This would catch anything small missed in previous interactions. Sometimes customers had questions they wanted answered, but were too distracted to ask. If there was a problem we could alert support immediately to step in and settle the matter before the issue escalated to something bigger.

Competitors may copy and reenact our key interactions, but they will never repeat the interactions to a similar standard.

> MAKE INTERACTIONS LOW-TOUCH

A low touch flow is typified by interactions that require little or no human input from the startup.

The advantage of a low touch system is that not only does it make the buying decision faster for the customer, but means the business can handle more sales volume, without adding more salesforce. Low touch are easier to measure, script and automate. With each customer requiring less time from the salesforce, the cost of acquiring a customer falls and profit rises.

It is likely your startup will begin with high touch interactions, and as the flow improves, introduce low touch activities. Until you get to product-market fit, company activities are inefficient because you are trying to figure out how to make a customer.

Another way to implement a low touch system is to begin high touch in the early game and move towards low touch interactions as the customer approaches the endgame. The first interaction can be an in-person meeting, the next interaction an internet conference call and the next interaction an online payment.

The mistake is to start high touch and stay high touch. Simply, the more we practice high touch, the better we become at it. It works, so why stop? An example of a high touch interaction is meeting a customer over coffee. It is high touch because the meeting is in person. The meeting day, time and location need to be planned, meaning lots of communication is exchanged. Then there's the travel time back and forth.

Shifting the salesforce and founder to low touch can be met with resistance. As soon as someone asks you to close deals over the phone, or tells you to invite the customer to your office, you're uncomfortable. It's boring. The idea of a salesperson being desk bound is preposterous. Customers deserve a one-to-one in-person experience. Anyway, it's liberating to get out of the office and unshackle yourself from the desk for a few hours.

The dilemma is high touch works, but it is not scalable. Everyday you practice high touch, just makes you better at high touch. Shift to low touch and you will lose deals because you and your sales team are making a transition and learning new skills.

> THICKEN THE EARLY GAME

Before designing a customer flow you have to make decisions about where your startup stands in the lifecycle. If you're a startup with less than three years of operating history, you are more likely to be in customer development. Customer development is concerned with learning how to make a customer, rather than making a customer.

Steve Blank, in his book *The Four Steps to Epiphany,* explains that customer development is an endeavor to discover how to make a customer. During customer development, sales are not important. It is learning how a sale is made that is important. Thicken the early game.

Startups are better off designing a customer flow that thickens the early game, particularly because they don't know a lot about Quadrant 1, and they have yet to validate whether benefits derived from Quadrant 2 solve customer problems.

A visitor arrives at your website anonymously. Analytics tell you the last page they clicked through from, their IP address, and what device they are using. However, you don't know which customer profile they belong to, nor their associated attitudes. So you need to keep an open mind and try a variety of value propositions to tease this intel out of the customer, without the customer feeling they are being profiled.

This strategy casts a wide net in the early game, and in the middle game, sees flows continue to converge as we near the endgame. The design of the flow resembles an arrowhead.

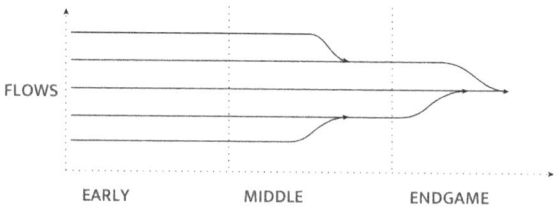

Each time you add a value proposition, you start a new flow. It has the effect of breaking down all the walls around the business and allows customers to charge into the business like cattle. This strategy boosts leads while making it possible to gather intel to make the next sale easier.

By tweaking value propositions, you can create messages which speak to different customer profiles and variants.

Likewise, it helps to have augmented Quadrant 2. With more products to offer, you can start a dialogue in a different way. Create as many propositions as possible. I recommend at least five propositions to discern what works and what doesn't work.

Here are a few examples of value propositions to create a customer in the early game.

Value proposition	Attitude	Temperature
Jump the queue	I'm ready to get started ASAP.	boiling
Get 15 minutes more with your practitioner	I'm ready to visit the clinic and remedy my ailment.	hot
Request a quote	I'm ready to share the fee with other decision makers.	warm
Sign up and get news	I'm ready to talk next year.	cold

Which value proposition a customer responds to can tell you about the customer's prevailing attitude and the temperature of a customer i.e., how ready are they are to buy today. Their choice of proposition becomes a means of qualifying the customer for the middle game. The higher the temperature, the more likely they will make a buying decision today and accept an express journey.

> CUSTOMER DEVELOPMENT IS INEFFICIENT

During consulting work I did for a cross-border payments company in Singapore, I designed an early game with five different ways to create a customer in the early game.

The operations manager reviewed the design. Here is a transcript of our discussion:

> **Operations:** Woooow! How are we going to manage this? We will have customers coming at us from all directions.
>
> **Me:** What customers?
>
> **Operations:** The customers who be pinging us
>
> **Me:** We have no customers today, so why will that change tomorrow?

Do not assume you will have lots of customers. Unless you're Instagram and growing at 20,000 new users a day like they did during their first few months of operation, you won't have a problem of "too many customers."

The reality for most startups is they are glad to get one customer, by any means necessary. If you have 20 ways of creating a customer and you get one customer through one of those means, you ought to celebrate.

Cast your mind back to Quadrant 1 and remember you are not obliged to serve everybody. Profiles you serve tomorrow and profiles you do not serve have to be dealt with appropriately and prevented from reaching the middle game. The key is not to block the customer but squeeze them out.

During my term at Futurebooks, we offered immigration services for foreigners moving to Singapore. Some customers mistook our immigration services for career opportunities. For this reason, we often received inquiries from individuals looking for work in Singapore. We explained to customers we did not offer this service.

We did not count these inquiries as customers we serve today, rather we counted them as a customer we served tomorrow. We monitored this customer profile and kept lists of names of these customers, until such day as we did have a product to match the profile.

Squeeze the early game. Squeeze out profiles you don't serve today. Then go to work on converting those that fit the customer profile you serve today. This has the effect of driving up your conversion rates in the middle and endgame. You narrow the field to make it easier for the salesforce to serve real customers.

> THICKEN THE MIDDLE GAME

If you are an established business with more than three years of operating history that has reached product-market fit, you are optimizing the early game and thickening the middle game. Marc Andreessen, Silicon Valley investor and co-founder of Netscape, coined the phrase, "product-market fit". It can be said that a startup with 40 percent of customers voicing that the product is a "must-have" signifies the company has reached product-market fit[9].

Startups with more experience and a better picture of the 4Qs can hone the early game to a few common ways to start a dialogue, and create more flows in the middle game. The design of the flow is more akin to a bloated fish.

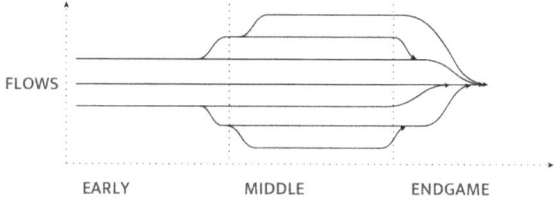

To thicken the middle game requires experience in Quadrant 1. Based on what you know about the customer's profile – goals, buying triggers, and attitudes – you can begin to map different journeys for each customer. Where Quadrant 3 has to be generic to work across many customer profiles,

Quadrant 4 can offer each customer profile and each product offer, a discrete experience.

The custom experience is created from a practice called qualifying, or triage. Think of triage like a fork in the road. At the fork, a traveler must choose a path. Each time they choose a path, they are routed to a different experience. Using techniques like conditional logic and smart forms, one can qualify, and continue to qualify a customer, adapting the experience to suit their choices.

With each interaction in the middle game, customers are qualified and routed into a unique track. It is imperative you have a thorough knowledge of Quadrant 1. Otherwise, your conditional logic will push customer profiles into the wrong flows. The last thing you want to do is win a customer in the early game, only to lose them in the middle by demonstrating how little you know about them. If you never understand the customer's attitudes, you cannot set up a customer correctly from the beginning, and the chances of closing a sale in the endgame are slim.

> SKIP THE MIDDLE GAME AND TAKE THE EXPRESS LANE

Most customers you will want to enter through the front door in the early game and leave via the back door in the endgame. Walking them through every interaction gives you the greatest chances of closing in the endgame.

The downside of this discipline is you could lose the customer in the middle game. It is not uncommon for 30% of customers to disappear in the middle game. Perhaps they have become busy making other types of buying decisions, or perhaps they have become snagged and ceased replying.

A solution is to short-circuit the flow and accomplish goals for some customers in fewer interactions. If you can build a flow that skips the middle game, you have fewer interactions to manage and therefore less friction.

Let's call this flow an express lane.

How do I get a customer into an express lane? From the moment you speak to customers you want to get a read on how urgently they want to buy. This is a customer whose temperature is high. This is a customer who has already past awareness and evaluation – they are ready to buy. They may be a more experienced buyer or are a repeat customer.

They have to tell you, and they tell you by their temperature, either because the customer responded to a certain type of value proposition indicating they have a higher temperature, or because they responded to two or more value propositions.

Customers who reply to a second or third value proposition are particularly vested. They have spent more time explaining their needs. Although not financial, they have made a small deposit into the relationship. They know from experience providing more information gets things moving.

A customer who drops off at the first interaction has a low temperature compared to a customer who completes all three interactions. It is a fine balance. It takes experience and timing to get a customer to skip the middle game. Forcing a customer into an express lane risks casting yourself as the overzealous salesperson.

> AVOID BEG MAIL

Earlier we said that it is not uncommon for 30 percent of customers to disappear in the middle game. One of the reasons the statistic is so high is because startups run out of value propositions and surrender to beg mail.

Beg mail commences once the initial consultation has taken place. After successfully making contact, establishing the company's credentials in the early game, and delivering an awesome proposal, quotation or demonstration in the middle game, the salesforce begins pestering the customer with beg mail.

Beg mail is where the salesforce call or messages a customer and beg for a decision. Instead of thickening the middle game, they shake down the middle game. They resort to high-pressure sales techniques to close the deal, or they beg the customer for a decision.

Tom made this mistake earlier with Sally, when he ran out of value mail, and instead, sent her bag mail.

During 2016 we friction tested several umbrella companies in the U.K. Umbrella companies provide shared services to contractors taking assignments from employers. We tested the strength of each competitor's middle game. We wanted to see what communications competitors would resort to after the first key interaction was over.

70 percent of competitors fired beg mail in the middle game. Worse still half of these competitors used automated beg mail. On day two, four and five of the friction test, we received precisely the same script, begging for a decision.

 Good Afternoon,

> I hope you are keeping well. I just wanted to send you a quick email to ensure that you received my email and to answer any questions that you may have in this regard.
>
> I look forward to your response.
>
> Best wishes,
>
> Zoe

Beg mail ruins any credibility built in the early game. I have seen salesforce fire bulk beg mail to an entire group of customers in the middle game. In the click of a button, they kill any chance of an endgame.

Sometimes beg mail is disguised as a follow-up call. The first chaser email sent to the customer is a legitimate follow-up. Every follow-up thereafter is a beg mail.

A salesforce that sends value mail has the advantage. They have thickened the middle game and began sending targeted communication. This organization stays top of mind, standing out from the pack as being valuable, honest and confident.

Competitors bombard the customer with beg mail fade out and become background noise. The more beg mail they fire at the customer, the more credibility their organization destroys.

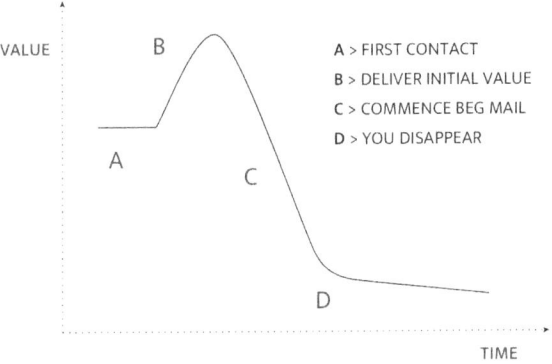

> KICK A GOAL IN THE ENDGAME

An endgame begins with a key interaction that signals the customer is ready to buy: a booking, payment of a deposit, signing an agreement to name a few.

Admission to the endgame is an important interaction because those in the endgame are expected to become a customer. This is the gateway to the business. Who will you let in and who will be refused?

In earlier stages, we have whittled out customer profiles we don't serve and put customers into the correct flows. We have served customers a product fact sheet from Quadrant 2, struck shared beliefs in Quadrant 3 and helped customers achieve their goal before expiry in the Quadrant 4.

An endgame closes with final interaction defining the moment the prospect becomes a customer.

In a consulting business, a customer may be defined when a contract for a scope of services is signed. For a SaaS startup, the definition of a customer could be the moment a payment is made to start a subscription.

Making a payment is not the sole definition of when a prospect turns to a customer. It could be when the prospect signs up for a 14-day free trial. Or perhaps it is when the prospect has achieved customer success. The metric for customer success could be a customer who has uploaded five transactions or completed 80 percent of the onboarding.

If we have done our job correctly, we have set ourselves up for an awesome endgame.

> AVOID FUDGING THE ENDGAME

An indiscretion among some sales people is to waive the final interaction in the endgame. They want to speed things up for the customer and get their bonus sooner by fudging the endgame. However, doing so puts the customer and business in jeopardy.

An example of a fudged endgame is one where the final customer interaction is a payment. The customer calls the consulting company who has been engaged to provide business advisory. The customer explains the check for the services has been cut and dispatched by mail. Although the sales agent knows the policy is that funds must be received before commencing services, they go ahead and make the prospect a customer.

Five days later the check has not arrived. The finance department calls the customer to chase payment. The customer explains they sent it and services have started. Finance is perplexed because only parties who have made payment can be a customer.

Ten days later the company is without payment and has provided 10 days of value with no remuneration.

The sales agent calls the customer to discuss how a payment can be made. The customer interrupts and changes the subject. They want to talk about an onboarding issue they are having with the service which is costing their business time and money. The last thing on the customer's mind is the payment.

When the definition of the customer is blurred, the customer experiences a rocking motion between being a prospect and a customer. Make it black and white. No matter the reason, a prospect must satisfy the requirement of the final interaction before being classed a customer.

> Q4 TAKEAWAYS

- 👉 equity from Q4 is far more defensible than equity from Q2

- 👉 if the delivery in Q4 is superior the customer will decide Q2 is superior

- 👉 tap Q4's irrational buying forces that eclipse the rational buying forces found in Q2

- 👉 calculate the number of interactions required to create a customer

- 👉 the fewer interactions you manage the less friction you are likely to introduce

- ☆ new players: white-label Q2 and focus equity in Q4 by finding new channels to host customer interactions and creating express lanes

- ★ existing players: identify a handful of key interactions in Q4 and split out these key interactions into more interactions, creating new experiences

- ▶ watch the 4Qs Insight, *SaaS customer onboarding mistakes*

THE 4Qs IN ACTION

I'm so glad you have got this far. You have at least an appreciation for the 4Qs. Although this book is written to be a conceptual guide, I do want to illustrate the 4Qs in action.

It will give you a sense of how this can be a decision-making tool, used by real people in real situations. As we roll through an example, watch the concepts come to life and refer to previous chapters to refresh your memory.

Before we get started, let's recap what we have learned.

Q1

> Who you serve today
> Who you serve tomorrow
> Who you never serve
> Thin slice
> Create buying triggers

Q2

> Avoid future-sell
> Name limits
> Offer work-arounds
> Defer customization
> Augment product

Q3

> Deliver a consistent brand
> Avoid becoming a Q2 fanatic
> Share beliefs
> Partners dilute shared beliefs
> Seize one customer profile

Q4

> Serve customers faster
> Nail key interactions
> Thicken the early game
> Thicken the middle game
> Kick a goal in the endgame

If you are clear on all the 4Qs, continue. Imagine you are made founder of a startup. The startup has been operating for three years and making sales providing Software-as-a-Service payroll to businesses. You decide to rollout the 4Qs to the entire company.

The first thing you do is benchmark the startup against competing sales systems. By friction testing the startup and its competitors, you can assess which quadrants you dominate and ones where there is room for improvement.

It has been two weeks since you ordered an audit. Here are the results of your friction test.

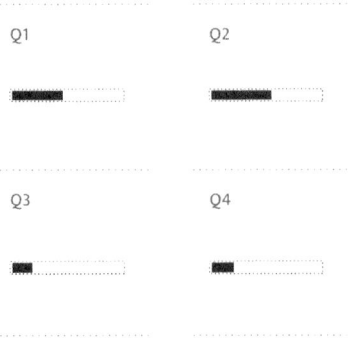

No surprise here. You're a technically-led founder and love spending your day tinkering with the product, so you created equity in Quadrants 1 and 2. We will need to do a lot of work in the remaining quadrants if you want to take the lead in the market.

Next we assign staff to different quadrants based on

their experience and preferences. We pop you into Quadrants 1 and 2. From here you can keep an eye on your creative baby in Quadrant 2 and have a say over who you will serve in Quadrant 1. To free you from a sales role, we have got others to support you and take up responsibility in Quadrants 3 and 4.

We don't want just any person. As Jim C. Collins remarked in his book *Good to Great*, we are looking to,

> Get the right people on the bus first.

We want the right people behind the 4Qs. People who want to cooperate to drive down friction and increase the odds a customer will write a positive review. Let's assemble our dream team and get them contributing to the 4Qs.

Tom requires no introduction. He is the sales guy. Tom spots new customer profiles and builds pipelines of customers to serve today and tomorrow. Tom is involved in delivering the experience in Quadrant 4. Since the team worked out who they serve, and who they don't serve, Tom has gained clarity, and become quite convincing on sales calls.

> You are our perfect customer. We exist to serve you.

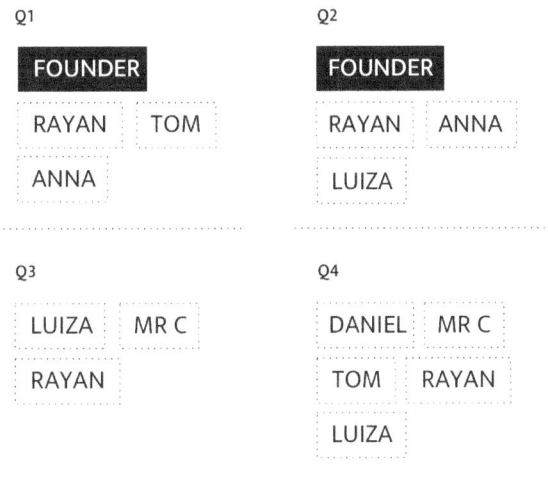

Tom made his mark on the business when he logged a piece of intel recently, changing the startup for the better. Tom discovered a new customer profile.

Since then, people regard him as a sort of hero. However, Anna eyes Tom judiciously during meetings. Tom has been caught on occasion future selling. It's sent her and her team into a tailspin trying to play catch up and build a product that frankly doesn't exist. Since Anna put in place a product fact sheet, Tom has been a lot easier to deal with and his attempts to future sell have been quelled.

Anna is the product manager. While she is most at home in Q2 where she can dabble in creating new products and features, Anna also crosses over to Q1. Anna and her team played a big part delivering requirements to meet Tom's initiative to serve a new customer profile. Anna finds herself firmly but politely reminding Tom and others that product doesn't fall out of the sky.

66 This ain't tech on tap.

Anna is aware changes to Q2 have longer cycle times compared to changes in any of the other three quadrants. So Anna is keen to learn how products serve customers, and the kinds of features they need to start thinking about to serve customers tomorrow.

Anna is talking to people from sales and marketing for the first time. Before the 4Qs was rolled out, she avoided them whenever possible. It was a bumpy road, but she is pleasantly surprised that she and Tom have become best buddies. During sales calls, Tom affectionately refers to Anna and her team as the wizards.

She has also struck up a relationship with Luiza, who lends a hand in guiding the design of product.

Luiza is an inhouse designer. Luiza has the eye of a hawk. She likes to watch how the company brands each of its interactions, and dutifully steps in when people "get off-brand".

She knows sales guys like Tom like to sneak out their own materials and without proper approval. At times it has made her unpopular. Luiza has had screaming matches with those who neglect to interpret the brand guideline correctly.

66 Why doesn't anyone read the brand guideline?!

Luiza recently gleaned a new perspective. She realized it wasn't because her team didn't read the guideline, it was because they didn't get it. She wrote a new version of the brand guideline, in friendly, easy-to-understand language. Luiza still shouts at people, but not as often.

Luiza spends some of her day moving the needle in Q2. She believes the product needs to look and feel just like the packaging. So she meets once a week with Anna to talk about improvements.

Luiza's big contribution to the 4Qs is achieving consistency in Quadrant 3, and creating new elements within the brand guideline for new types of interactions the startup have with customers. She and Daniel take lunch regularly, discussing how to improve the look of interactions taking place in Quadrant 4.

Her efforts have not gone unnoticed. Tom commented to the founder that conversion rates from the early-to-middle, and middle-to-endgame were all up. It seems since they rebranded and made all the interactions consistent, it is easier for the salesforce to do their job.

Daniel is a gifted WordPress developer. He is trying to make the experience for customers frictionless and onboard them into the product with the least number of interactions. Daniel spends his day improving the online experience in Quadrant 4.

What has been keeping Daniel awake at night is the online payments. Every interaction is under Daniel's control, except online payment. Online payment is looked after by a partner. At the time is seemed like a swell idea: outsource these interactions to a partner so the startup didn't have to concern themselves with the build.

> Their payment system works, but it's full of friction.

That's what Daniel told Rayan, after Rayan sat him down and demanded to know why the online payment interactions were taking so long to build. Daniel is not happy with the customer experience. It works, but it introduces unnecessary friction. Also, the partner promised the product could be white-labeled, but not to the extent Daniel first thought.

It dawned on Rayan that they hadn't assessed how the partner would fit into their vision of the 4Qs. Now they were stuck with them. Poor Daniel was spending his days educating their tech team about how to create a Quadrant 4.

Rayan made a call and spoke to the owner of the partner providing the online payment system. He was a nice fellow, and really wanted to help. After a few moments on the phone, Rayan knew they had little in common. The two firms held beliefs, none of which were shared. In the style of a Quadrant 2 fanatic, the owner reiterated how the product was the best on the market. Security, reliability, price. It didn't help that the partner's logo is plastered throughout the experience – a logo that frankly looked like it had been created by a preschooler.

Rayan put down the phone.

〝 I'm dealing with a Quadrant 2 fanatic.

He and Daniel agreed to give the partner another week, and if the partner didn't pick up the game, they were going with Plan B. Plan B was to send couriers to pick up the funds directly. It was not efficient but at least it eliminated a dependency and would get them end-to-end control of Quadrant 4.

Ah, now let's talk about Rayan. Rayan is a creative like Luiza. He is a copywriter by training. While Luiza produces the pictures, it is Rayan who produces the words. Together the two produce all the words and pictures for every customer interaction. Fixed to the wall behind Rayan's desk is a curious looking handwritten diagram. The diagram runs the entire length of the wall, spanning over three meters, with several sheets of A3 paper attached together.

Each of the interactions is fixed to the sheet of paper with semi-permanent tape. Some interactions are a sticky note. Luiza and Rayan sit around the diagram, creating words and pictures for new interactions and replacing outdated interactions. It is antiquated, but it serves their purpose.

Tom has put a lot of pressure on the team to chase a new customer profile. Serving the new profile isn't as easy as Tom thinks. The new customer profile has some special requirements. Rayan and Luiza had to design a new set of interactions to cater to the new profile. Rayan adjusted his view and took another look at the new sticky notes that had been added to the early game.

On the organizational chart, Rayan sits towards the bottom of the pecking order. However, within the realm of 4Qs, Rayan is more akin to a god. You see, Rayan is the customer experience officer. Rayan represents the customer we serve, the customer we serve tomorrow, the customer we are compelled to serve, and the customer we serve through.

Day and night he thinks about what it feels like to become a customer of our startup (Quadrant 4). Just the other week, Rayan forced Anna to roll back a new feature because it introduced too much friction. There were too many limits and naming those limits wasn't going to help.

> **❝ I'm not staying back every night for the next fortnight dealing with customer fallout.**

It hasn't always been easy for Rayan to get Anna's buy-in. The product team has an attitude where they want marketing kept out of product. That hadn't worked for Rayan. He and Tom designed a superior experience for the customer in the early, middle and endgame. However, that same experience did not extend into the product. The customer made the transaction and once they got to the unboxing, the whole experience collapsed.

The customers came back to Rayan and Tom, blaming them personally.

> **❝ You sold me on this. It is your fault.**

And it was their fault. Tom and Rayan would serve customers a product they knew wouldn't meet expectations. Rayan winced every time he heard the cash register open.

Since the 4Qs were implemented, the barrier between product and marketing has been torn down. Everyone can now see from the customer's point of view, the two are one and the same. That was a big victory for the company. Today the startup gets more positive reviews and even elicits reviews from customers who never bought the product.

Last week it was Rayan's turn to play the hero. He got everyone's attention when he tabled why they should cease serving two of four customer profiles.

"Honestly, this customer is a liability."

He had gathered intelligence which showed two profiles they served today, never wrote positive reviews. Everyone agreed unanimously to block the two profiles. Come Monday morning, they would announce a price increase that would have the effect of flushing out this profile.

Sales took a hit for three months, but today the business is back in shape. It turns out the two remaining customer profiles begin to consume more of the product. Explaining the results to the founder, Tom credits Rayan for the recovery. With fewer customer profiles to serve, Tom is doing a better job serving customers. Anna's team fast-tracked a few product features for the two remaining profiles. This meant Tom didn't have to name as many limits, driving down friction in the middle game.

Rayan also coached Tom on not sending beg mail, particularly in the middle game. Tom is grateful he doesn't have to beg for business anymore. He can triumphantly march into a meeting with a customer and have an interaction that builds trust, not one that undermines it. Like Luiza's initiative to brand every interaction consistently, avoiding beg mail made closing the endgame easier.

The strategy laid down by Rayan and the founder is one of thickening the early game. The startup has not reached product-market fit, and Rayan is not prepared to take a risk and assume they know how to create a customer. Daniel maintains seven different ways to make a customer – that's seven flows, each with their own sequence of interactions.

It keeps Tom glued to his cell phone and desktop PC. Tom can't leave the computer to visit the lavatory, and when he does, he asks Rayan or Luiza to watch the various screens. Tom has three screens at his desk. He watches leads come into the CRM application, a small desktop mounted tablet where he chats online to customers, and a mobile device he uses to receive and make calls.

> **❝ I'm really looking forward to product-market fit, or whatever you lot call it.**

He knows Rayan won't optimize the early game until they do. After work hours, Rayan spreads shared beliefs. He spends his evenings pottering about in Quadrant 3 and talking to you, the founder about what we share in common with customers. He chuckles, thinking about a fireside chat he and you shared one evening. It was late and the two of you had a few whiskeys and the topic got introspective.

❝ Why do we deserve to serve the customer?

He writes a lot of communications each day to customers, staff and partners. He exposes all of these profiles to the company's shared beliefs. He and you agree your next staff member might be a customer. Or your next customer might be a partner.

Last but not least, there is Mr C. Yes, that's right. The author of this book to whom you have patiently given your time plays a cameo role. As the founder you've asked him to step in and steward Quadrants 3 and 4, until someone experienced is hired.

❝ The person who logs the most intel gets a bottle of wine.

If you were ever going to free yourself from a sales role, others must log intel. A big part of a sales role is not only making a sale but making the next sale easier. To do this, the salesforce collects intel. Tom is an early adopter. In the first week alone he logs 20 pieces of intelligence, including one ticket which leads to the discovery of a new customer profile, one which the competition is not serving. It earned Tom a rep as being a bit of a hero.

Let's trace the footsteps of this ticket; where it began and eventually how it became words and pictures, and how one piece of intel transformed the startup.

It all began with a sales meeting. Tom went and met a customer to gather requirements and demo the product. It was a recruitment company. The company employed contract staff on behalf of large local and foreign firms. The contractors were geographically spread out. Collecting accurate time and attendance data from this type of workforce was manual and wages were always paid late. There were frequent disputes over wage computations with contractors.

If the time and attendance data could be improved, the customer would buy their payroll application. However, without better time and attendance data, their payroll application was no better than what the customer used currently. Tom fondled the ID badge that hung around his neck and recounted the words Rayan had said.

❝ Don't future sell. Don't future sell.

Tom wanted the deal so bad, but he knew if he tried to serve the customer, he'd future-sell and ruin any trust he'd built. Instead of going back to his desk to write a quote, Tom sat in the back of the taxi, logging the find on the intel board. Tom didn't have the answer, but he was sure one of his team would.

He wrote to a colleague and asked that they conduct a market analysis of recruitment companies. You needed to know the size of their contractor count, if their customer were foreign or local businesses, to try to build a picture of the customer profile. That week you struck gold. One of the largest HR events in the country was being staged. So Tom attended, snooping around trade booths, squirreling-away business cards, and observing how this customer profile behaved. He logged more intel.

Rayan read Tom's tickets as they surfaced. Rayan and the founder were the first to read any intel that appeared on the board. While Tom was at the event, Rayan decided to friction test their competitors. It had been a few months since their last friction test and he was keen to learn if any competitors served the recruitment companies. They didn't. Rayan logged this intel.

Anna was on her way home when she saw the notifications on her phone. Her phone had been buzzing all afternoon and she resisted the temptation to read notifications. Sitting on the bus, she had all the time in the world to read. The intel board was hive of activity. Splashed across the tickets were the names of Rayan and Tom.

🙶 What the heck is going on?

One at time, Anna read the tickets. Tom had clearly articulated the problem. No matter how good the payroll application, if the time and attendance data were inaccurate, the payslips were inaccurate. All the payroll apps in the world were not going to solve this problem.

What Rayan and Tom didn't know was Anna and the founder had been working on a project to source a device that could gather time and attendance data, accurately. It was a prototype. She shared the schematics of the device on the ticket. Anna smiled inwardly as she hit save on the ticket. Tomorrow would be like starting the business all over again.

Rayan opened the meeting the next day and explained briefly the new customer profile and the fact they were underserved. Looking at the intel Tom and Rayan had logged, it was clear to the team that this was an opportunity they could not pass up.

Anna was grateful Tom hadn't future sold the company. If he had, there is no chance Anna could bail him out. Serving recruitment companies was a big commitment. They'd need to be firing on all quadrants if they were gonna make an impression. Instead, Tom used his time productively to gather intel. The fellow even had a fix on what the customer buying triggers looked like and likely buying date.

Anna proposed a solution the product team had been working on. It would mean the company would need to broaden its competency to include hardware, as well as software development.

The team decided this would be a customer they would serve tomorrow. Tom began calling recruitment companies, not serving them a product, but gathering their thoughts on the problem and Anna's proposed solution. A few campaigns later, and Tom had more intel. He even managed to signed up over a hundred customers to a waiting list to receive a notification once the feature was built. Way to go Tom.

Rayan tapped away at his keyboard. He could hear Tom making calls from the next room. Rayan ran the numbers on this customer profile. He wanted to be sure it was a profile they could economically serve. He was sure they could.

> Let's do this.

For the first time, she felt their decision-making was empirical. Anna held a dark secret. She believed 50 percent of what was built in Q2 was binned in a year. Today, she felt they had sufficient intel to support why her team should build the feature.

No one seemed bothered that you, the founder, were on holiday and that they would be making a decision without you. A month ago, they couldn't change a toilet roll without you.

Today, it felt natural to make a decision, and to hold each other accountable.

Intel was great, but intel was no use without action. If they were going to become a market leader, they needed to act like one.

Anna and Rayan had been busy the night before writing up briefs and planning exactly what projects needed to get done, the sequence of the projects and what quadrants they would hit. Everyone agreed there was no point in inviting more customers into the business until the underlying deficit in Quadrant 3 was addressed.

The first few projects needed to address the brand and how it applied to every interaction. If they got it right, sales would increase from the existing two profiles, as well as the new profile. In each Quadrant they plotted projects and the sequence. The persons assigned to the quadrant would take responsibility for the project and see it as delivered.

Anna calls you personally. She lets you know they put the device on steroids and pulled it up the product road map.

When you put the phone down you think long and hard. On the surface, the shareholders would discount your decision to take on the liability of managing hardware. They would not appreciate how augmenting Quadrant 2 would reinforce shared beliefs.

Since the time you started the company your single goal was to write a payroll application that was compliant. Part of being compliant was being accurate, and the device filled that gap.

Later in the week, Tom paid Anna an unscheduled visit. Tom liked to snoop in the kitchen to see what was cooking, and hope to catch some gossip on how a product or feature was coming along. Anna, tight-lipped, told him nothing.

> ❝ Get lost Tom, I'm not telling you anything.

Q1	Q2
D. RECRUITMENT FIRMS	E. NEW PRODUCT

Q3	Q4
A. BRAND OVERHAUL	C. ONLINE PAYMENT
	B. REBRAND INTERACTIONS
	F. ONBOARDING
	G. DELIVERY

Tom sighed and groaned like he did everytime she evaded his questions about when a product would be ready. The two were good friends now, so it became an ongoing joke. He'd ask when it would be ready. She'd reply to get lost. At best she said it would be ready in the fall.

Tom gave customers the impression he had connections in the organization and could pull strings to make features appear earlier. Unfortunately, it wasn't true. The truth was Tom was in the dark as much as customers about new features and products. He only found out when a feature was released around the same time customers were told.

Tom complained to the founder he needed access to the product roadmap.

When it came to the product road map and people interfering with it, Anna got ten times nastier than Luiza. Unlike the customer profile, brand guideline and customer flow, the product road map was tightly held secret. It was locked up in vault somewhere. If he ever got his hands on it, he'd have to go into witness protection.

Rayan had skipped the office most days that week. He had not been seen in his office and the customer flow that normally hung on the glass wall behind his desk was missing.

Rayan had locked himself away at a cafe he went to when he and Luiza needed to crank out words and pictures. He found it was the only place he could get anything done for an extended period. With his laptop perched in front of him and the customer flow spread-eagle across the table beside him, Rayan began designing the new interactions. Luiza joined him a few hours later, a sketch pad under her arm.

He punched away at the keyboard, not noticing her.

Rayan had become tired of one competitor in particular, stealing words and pictures he and Luisa so painstaking created. They picked up their value propositions, and repeated them verbatim. There wasn't a darn thing he could do to stop them. They copied everything – even their prices.

Rayan was certain the founder of the competing firm was a Quadrant 3 fanatic. Over beer the night before, Rayan shared his views with Tom. Years ago, Tom had worked for the competing firm.

Tom explained with a grin that the founder of the competing firm always sold the big picture and drove shared beliefs, but didn't recognize the product didn't live up to the image. Customers would call and complain, and it was Tom who had to take their calls. He seemed to be around to do the selling, but never around to deal with customer fallout.

Tom explained with a fervor that the same founder forgot what features the product did have and sold a version to a customer that wasn't in the warehouse. The tech team was expected to build the product and ship it the next day.

Tom put a paternal arm around Rayan's shoulder, reenacting the scenario and the founder's behavior.

> The leg has fallen off the chair.

> It doesn't matter if the leg has fallen off the chair. It's the color we care about.

Tom would call the customer, explain they'd been sold something that was not available and ask they wait three months until stock arrived. That made for really "happy" customers. They would bring customers into the company that had no business being here. It was almost cheaper if they paid the customer to leave.

It got so bad, the staff avoided talking to him about future releases of the product. Just having a conversation about a feature was an admission the feature had been built.

> I think at one point we had sold five different versions of the product. Talk about tech on tap.

Rayan brought his thoughts back to the present. Now that his team had a new customer profile, a new product coming and a bunch of other stuff happening in other quadrants, he wasn't so sure the competitor could copy their words and pictures. For the first time, they weren't talking about the same product category. They were talking in completely different terms, using new kinds of words and value propositions the competition was not familiar with.

By the time the competitors retraced and figured out the customer they were serving, they would be 100 or so iterations in front. When they made promises to customers they couldn't keep, Rayan's team would be there to collect.

> **They will react like they always do. They will follow like sheep and future sell.**

For so long Rayan and Luiza had reacted to the competition. Now the game was on their terms. It was beginning to feel rigged in their favor. Rayan could plot the journey of a customer, and how the competitor was one part of the master plan. The competitor helped educate the market, create unsatisfied customers and draw a distinction between companies that were followers and those that were leaders.

It was that last thought that was sobering. Becoming a leader would put them in a position for a price increase when all the competitors were busy slashing prices and undercutting.

A few more sentences sprang on the page as the writer in him typed away. Rayan leaned back on the chair and marveled over the page before him.

> **Steal this.**

TEACH ME HOW YOU APPLIED THE 4Qs

Would you mind dropping me a review today? I want to learn how you are using the 4Qs. Point your camera phone at the QR code and follow the link. When you arrive on the Amazon page, scroll down until you reach the product review section. I look forward to hearing from you!

ANTHONY COUNDOURIS

GRAB THE FREE 4Qs PLAYBOOK

Our playbook will teach you how to play or fit one Quadrant with another. Master a Quadrant 1-2, 1-3, and a 2-3 fit. Visit runfrictionless.com or point your camera phone at the QR code. Alternatively, you can access 4Qs templates from popular template sharing sites.

GLOSSARY

Sales system. A system involving intelligence gathering, 4Qs decision-making and creation of words and pictures.

Words and pictures. The exterior or veneer which customers and competitors experience.

Intel. Information gathered inside and outside the business which informs one of the four quadrants and leads to a reduction in friction.

4Qs. A framework for designing a sales system. Intelligence is gathered and synthesized to address one of four Quadrants.

Quadrant 1. Is about who the customer is – who we serve.

Quadrant 2. What we sell the customer – what we serve.

Quadrant 3. Sharing beliefs with the customer – who we are.

Quadrant 4. What it feels like to become a customer – how we serve.

Customer goal. The purpose of a sales system is to achieve the customer's goal in the shortest possible time.

Friction. Any obstacle which slows the customer reaching their goal, and equally slows the sale from occurring.

Friction test. A tool or method used to gather intelligence, test and benchmark the strength of a competing sales systems.

Drop-off. Occurs when a customer delays or abandons their goal. Drop-off is more likely to be avoided when this equation is satisfied: X (perceived product benefits) > Y (customer effort).

Customer success. A metric which measures when a customer has achieved their goal. Often the metric has non-monetary value.

Customer interaction. Occurs each time a customer comes into contact with the business.

Future sell. When someone in the startup commits the company to build a feature tomorrow, in order to make a sale today.

Startup. A company with less than three years operating history. Or a company with more than three years operating history, that thinks and moves like a startup.

Product. A product or service.

Salesforce. Every person in the startup responsible for serving a customer.

Partner. A third party licensing a technology for a startup to use in Quadrants 2 or 4.

Customer profile. A customer or prospect customer.

Customer expiry. The length of time in minutes, hours, days or months which a customer will seek a goal before dropping off.

Variant. A subset of a customer profile discovered after thin slicing.

Thin slicing. The act of breaking down customer profile into variants according to a significant data point such as attitudes or buying triggers.

Buying triggers. An event which triggers a customer profile or variant to make a buying decision.

Buying decision. Three phases which a customer experiences when deciding to buy a product. These phases are described within as the early, middle and endgame, and belong to Quadrant 4.

Value proposition. This is the promise made to a customer. A value proposition is comprised of a key message, a channel and a call-to-action.

Customer development. A phase of a startup's lifecycle where the startup experiences friction. Steve Blank explains customer development is an endeavor to discover how to make a customer.

Product-market fit. The formula by which a startup makes a predictable sale. Marc Andreessen, Silicon Valley investor and co-founder of Netscape, coined the phrase.

SaaS (Software as a Service) provider. A company offering customers subscription plans to customers over the internet.

Early, middle and endgame. Customer interactions are grouped into an early, middle and endgame, to make measuring conversion easier.

Conversion. The number or percentage of customers who convert from the early, to the middle and through to the endgame.

Key interactions. The few interactions which have the greatest impact on achieving the customer's goal.

JustPayroll. A provider of payroll software and payroll services to enterprise companies in the Philippines.

InstaSave. A cross-border payments provider for white-collar professionals headquartered in Singapore.

Phorest. A SaaS provider of management software for spa and salon businesses, headquartered in Ireland.

Futurebooks. An accounting and compliance company serving startups in Singapore.

Firestarter. A digital marketing agency serving enterprise customers in Singapore.

[1] Taylor, Frederick W. *The Principles of Scientific Management*. Cambridge: Harper & Brothers, 1911

[2] Brinker, Scott. "*Marketing Technology Landscape Supergraphic (2017): Martech 5000*." Chief Marketing Technologist Blog, last modified May 10, 2017. http://chiefmartec.com/2017/05/marketing-techniology-landscape-supergraphic-2017/

[3] "*Google Docs Help Forum*," last modified August 13, 2016, https://productforums.google.com/forum/#!topic/docs/KQaFFVGonV0

[4] "*Google Docs Help Forum*," last modified February 7, 2016, https://productforums.google.com/forum/#!topic/docs/VwNiGsNB34o

[5] BBC News, *"Cybertruck: Tesla truck gets 150,000 orders despite launch gaffe"* last modified 24 Nov 2019, https://www.bbc.com/news/business-50536200

[6] Isaacson, Walter. *Steve Jobs*. New York: Simon & Schuster, 2011

[7] Isaacson, Walter. *Steve Jobs*. New York: Simon & Schuster, 2011

[8] "*How Google's Powerful Lobby Legalized Driverless Cars In California*," Tech Crunch, last modified September 24, 2012, https://techcrunch.com/2012/09/24/how-googles-powerful-lobby-legalized-driverless-cars-in-california/

[9] "*Product-market fit*," Wikipedia, last modified June 6, 2018, https://en.wikipedia.org/wiki/Product/market_fit